PROSTATE CANCER

Anthrax

Antibiotic-resistant
 Bacteria

Avian Flu

Botulism

Campylobacteriosis

Cervical Cancer

Cholera

Ebola

Encephalitis

Escherichia coli
 Infections

Gonorrhea

Hantavirus Pulmonary
 Syndrome

Helicobacter pylori

Hepatitis

Herpes

HIV/AIDS

Infectious Fungi

Influenza

Legionnaires' Disease

Leprosy

Lung Cancer

Lyme Disease

Mad Cow Disease
 (Bovine Spongiform
 Encephalopathy)

Malaria

Meningitis

Mononucleosis

Pelvic Inflammatory
 Disease

Plague

Polio

Prostate Cancer

Rabies

Salmonella

SARS

Smallpox

Staphylococcus aureus
 Infections

Streptococcus
 (Group A)

Syphilis

Toxic Shock Syndrome

Tuberculosis

Tularemia

Typhoid Fever

West Nile Virus

PROSTATE CANCER

Scott D. Cramer, Ph.D.

FOUNDING EDITOR
The Late **I. Edward Alcamo**
Distinguished Teaching Professor of Microbiology,
SUNY Farmingdale

FOREWORD BY
David Heymann
World Health Organization

CHELSEA HOUSE
PUBLISHERS
An imprint of Infobase Publishing

Dedicated to Ed Alcamo

Prostate Cancer

Copyright © 2007 by Infobase Publishing

Chelsea House
An imprint of Infobase Publishing
132 West 31st Street
New York NY 10001

ISBN-10: 0-7910-8935-5
ISBN-13: 978-0-7910-8935-4

Library of Congress Cataloging-in-Publication Data
Cramer, Scott D.
   Prostate cancer / Scott D. Cramer ; foreword by David Heymann.
         p. cm. — (Deadly diseases and epidemics)
   Includes bibliographical references and index.
   ISBN 0-7910-8935-5 (hardcover)
   1. Prostate—Cancer—Juvenile literature. I. Title. II. Series.
   RC280.P7C73 2006
   619.99'463—dc22   2006024074

Chelsea House books are available at special discounts when purchased in bulk quantities for businesses, associations, institutions, or sales promotions. Please call our Special Sales Department in New York at (212) 967-8800 or (800) 322-8755.

You can find Chelsea House on the World Wide Web at http://www.chelseahouse.com

Series design by Terry Mallon
Cover design by Keith Trego

Printed in the United States of America

Bang EJB 10 9 8 7 6 5 4 3 2 1

This book is printed on acid-free paper.

All links and Web addresses were checked and verified to be correct at the time of publication. Because of the dynamic nature of the Web, some addresses and links may have changed since publication and may no longer be valid.

Personal profiles are reprinted with the permission of the contributors.

Proscar is a registered trademark of Merck. Taxotere is a registered trademark of Sanofi-Aventis US LLC.

Table of Contents

Acknowledgments

I would like to thank all of the men, women, and children who contributed their personal stories to this book. It is for them that this book is written. I would especially like to thank Darrell Bartlett and his wife, Lorna. Darrell was instrumental in providing the original idea for the personal profiles and he helped me recruit a number of other people. Without Lorna's help I would not have been in contact with the Banas family. The others that contributed, the Banas family, Katie Ruff, Norton Ernest, and Roxanne Cramer all deserve credit. It takes a dedicated spirit to confront the difficult issues that they all addressed. Finally, this book is dedicated to the memories of my stepfather, Stanley J. Odmann and my uncle Les Cramer.

Foreword

In the 1960s, many of the infectious diseases that had terrorized generations were tamed. After a century of advances, the leading killers of Americans both young and old were being prevented with new vaccines or cured with new medicines. The risk of death from pneumonia, tuberculosis (TB), meningitis, influenza, whooping cough, and diphtheria declined dramatically. New vaccines lifted the fear that summer would bring polio, and a global campaign was on the verge of eradicating smallpox worldwide. New pesticides like DDT cleared mosquitoes from homes and fields, thus reducing the incidence of malaria, which was present in the southern United States and which remains a leading killer of children worldwide. New technologies produced safe drinking water and removed the risk of cholera and other water-borne diseases. Science seemed unstoppable. Disease seemed destined to all but disappear.

But the euphoria of the 1960s has evaporated.

The microbes fought back. Those causing diseases like TB and malaria evolved resistance to cheap and effective drugs. The mosquito developed the ability to defuse pesticides. New diseases emerged, including AIDS, Legionnaires', and Lyme disease. And diseases which had not been seen in decades re-emerged, as the hantavirus did in the Navajo Nation in 1993. Technology itself actually created new health risks. The global transportation network, for example, meant that diseases like West Nile virus could spread beyond isolated regions and quickly become global threats. Even modern public health protections sometimes failed, as they did in 1993 in Milwaukee, Wisconsin, resulting in 400,000 cases of the digestive system illness cryptosporidiosis. And, more recently, the threat from smallpox, a disease believed to be completely eradicated, has returned along with other potential bioterrorism weapons such as anthrax.

The lesson is that the fight against infectious diseases will never end.

In our constant struggle against disease, we as individuals have a weapon that does not require vaccines or drugs, and that is the warehouse of knowledge. We learn from the history of science that "modern" beliefs can be wrong. In this series of books, for example, you will learn that diseases like syphilis were once thought to be caused by eating potatoes. The invention of the microscope set science on the right path. There are more positive lessons from history. For example, smallpox was eliminated by vaccinating everyone who had come in contact with an infected person. This "ring" approach to smallpox control is still the preferred method for confronting an outbreak, should the disease be intentionally reintroduced.

At the same time, we are constantly adding new drugs, new vaccines, and new information to the warehouse. Recently, the entire human genome was decoded. So too was the genome of the parasite that causes malaria. Perhaps by looking at the microbe and the victim through the lens of genetics we will be able to discover new ways to fight malaria, which remains the leading killer of children in many countries.

Because of advances in our understanding of such diseases as AIDS, entire new classes of antiretroviral drugs have been developed. But resistance to all these drugs has already been detected, so we know that AIDS drug development must continue.

Education, experimentation, and the discoveries that grow out of them are the best tools to protect health. Opening this book may put you on the path of discovery. I hope so, because new vaccines, new antibiotics, new technologies, and, most importantly, new scientists are needed now more than ever if we are to remain on the winning side of this struggle against microbes.

David Heymann
Executive Director
Communicable Diseases Section
World Health Organization
Geneva, Switzerland

Introduction

Prostate cancer is a deadly disease that affects millions of men each year. There are few people who have not been touched personally or through friends or family by this disease. Before the twentieth century it was hardly recognized as a disease by doctors. This year hundreds of thousands of men will be diagnosed with prostate cancer—unfortunately it happens every year. While prostate cancer is considered a disease of old men, it now can be found in middle-aged men.

This book is a guide for teenagers who have a father, uncle, grandfather, or friend who has prostate cancer. My intent is to explain the biology of the disease, how it is detected, and how it is treated. Also included is information on how prostate cancer may be prevented. There are no clear guidelines on prevention but there are some strong suggestions of what may help. It is hard for a teenager to imagine that what he does now could affect his prostate-cancer risk 40 years from now. But it could.

Another major goal of the book is to put a human face on prostate cancer. There are several profiles of men who have or had prostate cancer throughout the book. The range of profiles is meant to show how anybody can be affected, from a police officer, to a rock star, to a Nobel prize winner. Also included are essays written by people whose father or husband has or had prostate cancer. People have different perspectives on how to deal with a loved one who has prostate cancer, which can be helpful to read. These profiles are in the writers' own words.

The book can be technical and perhaps challenging in parts. I introduce terms that might be encountered in a discussion about the clinical aspects of prostate cancer. Some concepts, such as the hormonal control of prostate growth in chapter 6, are rather demanding and will likely require close attention. The referenced resources can enhance understanding of the scientific principles. The book describes the anatomy and reproductive functions of the prostate and states clearly the consequences of treatment strategies on reproductive function and sexual intercourse. Everyone should be aware of these real and important consequences of the disease.

As a guide for teenagers, this book is not intended as a tool for prostate cancer patients to make decisions about treatment strategies or interpretations of test results—decisions should be made in consultation with a qualified doctor. However, there is information that a patient and his family might find useful in preparation for a consultation with a doctor. The field of prostate cancer is rapidly evolving, and there are numerous resources that can aid in the latest decision-making options. Reliable resources are found in the Further Reading section, including Web sites, at the end of the book.

Scott D. Cramer, Ph.D.
April 7, 2006

1

What Is Prostate Cancer and Who Gets It?

Age, race, family history: These are the three well-known and accepted risk factors for prostate cancer.
Know them and you will know your risk.

Prostate cancer is the most common cancer in men in the United States, and the third leading cause of cancer death among men (lung and colon cancer are first and second, respectively). Age is the number-one risk factor for prostate cancer. The older a man gets, the more likely he will get prostate cancer. There are distinct racial differences in both the incidence of prostate cancer (the rate at which new cases are diagnosed) and in the death rate due to prostate cancer. There are clearly genetic factors that lead to prostate cancer. There are also lifestyle factors (environmental and dietary) that lead to prostate cancer. The disease does not discriminate against any man. Virtually all men are at risk for developing prostate cancer.

PROSTATIC DISEASES

The prostate is an organ located at the base of the bladder in male mammals; in the mature adult human male it is about the size of a walnut (see chapter 2 for more about prostate anatomy). There are three main diseases of the prostate. **Prostatitis** is inflammation of the prostate. Often this inflammation may be caused by bacterial or fungal infection, but may be caused by other factors. Typical symptoms can include pain in the rectum, testicles, bladder or penis, and pain during urination or ejaculation. There is no direct evidence that prostatitis is a precursor to prostate cancer or that it leads to prostate cancer. However, some investigators feel that some cancers, including prostate cancer, could be triggered by inflammation associated with infection.

Benign prostatic hyperplasia (**BPH**, sometimes referred to as benign prostatic hypertrophy) is a growth of the prostate unrelated to prostate cancer that affects the majority of elderly men. The word *hyperplasia* derives from the Greek words *hyper* and *plasia*, meaning overdevelopment or excess growth. BPH is an enlargement of the prostate gland caused by excess growth of glandular tissue, tightening the urethra and obstructing urination. The causes of BPH are unknown. Its main symptoms are associated with urination: Men with BPH have to urinate often and cannot completely evacuate their bladder of urine. The most common indication of BPH is the need to get up often during the night to urinate. BPH is a huge medical problem in the United States, resulting in billions of dollars spent on associated health care. Some people estimate that as many as 60 percent of men at age 60 have some form of BPH, 70 percent of men at age 70, 80 percent of men at age 80, and so on. The first symptoms of BPH may show up in men as young as 40 to 50 years old. In severe cases of BPH, there can be associated bladder problems and even kidney infections. As with prostatitis, there is no evidence that BPH is a precursor of or leads to prostate cancer.

Prostate cancer is an aggressive growth of malignant cancerous cells in the prostate that can be fatal. The causes of prostate cancer are not completely understood, but this book will focus on some major research into its causes. Often the diagnosis of prostate cancer occurs from routine annual screening, before there are any physical signs. However, symptoms of prostate cancer can vary from none to painful urination, blood in the urine, bone pain, muscle weakness, and others.

Table 1.1 **Leading Sites of New Cancer Cases and Deaths in Men and Women, 2006 Estimates**

ESTIMATED NEW CASES		ESTIMATED DEATHS	
Male	**Female**	**Male**	**Female**
Prostate 234,460 (33%)	Breast 212,920 (31%)	Lung and bronchus 90,330 (31%)	Lung and bronchus 72,130 (26%)
Lung and bronchus 92,700 (13%)	Lung and bronchus 81,770 (12%)	Prostate 27,870 (10%) Breast	Colon 40,970 (15%)
Colon and rectum 72,800 (10%)	Colon and rectum 75,810 (11%)	Prostate 27,350 (9%)	Colon and rectum 27,300 (10%)
Urinary bladder 44,690 (6%)	Uterine corpus 41,200 (6%)	Pancreas 16,090 (6%)	Pancreas 16,210 (6%)
Melanoma of the skin 34,260 (5%)	Non-Hodgkin's lymphoma 28,190 (4%)	Leukemia 12,470 (4%)	Ovary 15,310 (6%)
Non-Hodgkin's lymphoma 30,680 (4%)	Melanoma of the skin 27,930 (4%)	Liver and intrahepatic bile duct 10,840 (4%)	Leukemia 9,810 (4%)
Kidney and renal pelvis 24,650 (3%)	Thyroid 22,590 (3%)	Esophagus 10,730 (4%)	Non-Hodgkin's lymphoma 8,840 (3%)
Oral cavity and pharynx 20,180 (3%)	Ovary 20,180 (3%)	Non-Hodgkin's lymphoma 10,000 (3%)	Uterine corpus 7,350 (3%)
Leukemia 20,000 (3%)	Urinary bladder 16,730 (2%)	Urinary bladder 8,990 (3%)	Multiple myeloma 5,630 (2%)
Pancreas 17,150 (2%)	Pancreas 16,580 (2%)	Kidney and renal pelvis 8,130 (3%)	Brain and other nervous system 5,560 (2%)
All sites 720, 280 (100%)	All sites 679,510 (100%)	All sites 291,270 (100%)	All sites 273,560 (100%)

*Excludes basal and squamous cell skin cancers and in situ carcinoma except urinary bladder

Note: Percentages are approximate.

Source: American Cancer Society. "Cancer Facts and Figures 2006." Available online. URL: http://www.cancer.org/. Accessed June 5, 2006.

PROSTATE CANCER IS COMMON

Prostate cancer is the most common tumor in men (excluding skin cancer). The sheer number of men affected by prostate cancer makes it unusual for a person not to know someone affected by this serious, sometimes fatal disease. The rate at which new cases of cancer are diagnosed is called the incidence rate, and the rate at which people die from a cancer is the mortality rate. The American Cancer Society estimates that for 2006 there will be about 234,000 new cases of prostate cancer in the United States (see Table 1.1). The second most common cancer in men is lung (93,000), followed by cancer of the colon and rectum (73,000), bladder (45,000), non-Hodgkin's lymphoma (31,000), kidney (25,000), mouth (esophagus, larynx) (20,000), leukemia (20,000), and pancreas (17,000).

Prostate cancer is the third leading cause of cancer death in men, after lung and colon cancers. The American Cancer Society estimates that there will be 90,000 deaths in men due to lung cancer in 2006, 27,000 from colon and rectal, 27,000 from prostate, 16,000 from pancreatic, 12,000 from leukemia, 11,000 from liver, 11,000 from esophageal, 10,000 from non-Hodgkin's lymphoma, 9,000 from bladder, and 8,000 from kidney cancer.[1]

When we compare the cancer incidence rate to the cancer mortality rate, it is clear that certain cancers are much more deadly than others. Lung cancer and pancreatic cancer are very deadly. New cases of lung cancer among men are predicted to be 93,000 and 90,000 men are expected to die from the disease. Of the 17,000 new cases of pancreatic cancer, 16,000 men will die from complications of the disease, usually within the first six months after diagnosis. It is difficult to diagnose these cancers until they are very advanced, and then it is too late.

Prostate cancer has a more favorable outcome. Compare the numbers: 234,000 predicted new cases of prostate cancer in 2006, with only 27,000 predicted deaths from the disease. The reasons for this are complex, but have to do with the less

ONE FAMILY'S EXPERIENCE

Prostate cancer affects the entire family. This profile of the Banas family and their experiences with Ron Banas' prostate cancer highlights their struggle and strength as a family and as individuals.

ROBBIE BANAS, OLDEST SON, 16 YEARS OLD

My father has always been an integral part of my life. It was devastating when I learned that he was diagnosed with prostate cancer. I was contemplating what would happen to the family with my father so ill with cancer.

When I went to the hospital after my dad's surgery, I was in a panic not knowing what to expect. I went to see him for the first time the evening after his surgery. He was in a lot of pain and was hooked up to monitoring equipment. It was upsetting to see him in this condition. He was in the hospital for five days. I saw improvement in his condition each day. Then I was overcome with joy to see that all was going to be fine and he could return home.

I am an avid swimmer today because of the years of lessons provided by my father. He was a great fan and supported all my sports. He was at soccer, basketball and baseball games to constantly cheer me on.

I firmly believe in the power and strength of prayer. As a result, I religiously pray to God that my father will be a prostate cancer survivor. I hope he will be there to give me guidance, support, and love. I love my father dearly, and desperately need him to be a part of my life. My entire family is counting on my father to provide for our well-being, both now and in the future.

KYLE BANAS, YOUNGEST SON, 11 YEARS OLD.

I felt very sad when I learned that my father has prostate cancer. I found out about his cancer from my mother. She told me he was going to have surgery in December. I was also very worried and scared.

Figure 1.1 The Banas family (clockwise from left: Kyle, Ron, Robbie, Susan). Courtesy the Banas family.

My family spent Christmas Day at the hospital by my father's bed. While other families were enjoying the holiday, I was just hoping that my dad would get better and come home soon.

I realized that I needed help from God. I requested that special prayers be said for my dad at my religious class. Every night I prayed before going to sleep. It is my belief that this helped because my father survived the prostate surgery.

I will continue my prayers in the hope that he will be a survivor. I love my dad with all my heart and soul. I hope he has good health forever.

SUSAN BANAS, WIFE AND MOTHER

My husband, Ron, has prostate cancer. I have known my husband since I was 19 years old. Ron did not have any symptoms of his prostate cancer. Many members of his family have died from various types of cancer, so he always went for a yearly checkup. This year, his PSA test indicated that the level was a 13. He had a biopsy the following week. The doctor called him at work to let him know that six out of the seven pieces of tissue were malignant. Ron called me immediately at work and my initial reaction was one of extreme sadness. I began to cry at the desk in my office.

It has now been four months since his initial diagnosis. The words and emotions that have gone through my mind in dealing with this condition include anger, shock, fear, uncertainty, inspiration, and hope.

Anger: I feel angry that this has happened to my husband. My husband had surgery on December 22· and I spent Christmas at the hospital with my children.

Shock: I often lie awake at night and still cannot believe that this cancer has occurred in our lives. I often wish the clock could be turned back to before this all began to happen.

Fear: I am afraid each time he has a blood test that his PSA level will be higher. This will force us to make new decisions that will, I hope, be correct. I fear for the future and hope my children do not have any symptoms of this cancer lurking in their genes.

Uncertainty: My husband often tells me that he wonders if this will be his last spring or summer. Cancer throws an uncertainty into your life because you do not know when it will return. I have two sons, ages 11 and 16. I hope he will be alive to attend their graduations and weddings.

I also hope we can grow old together without the pain of this disease.

Inspiration: The positive side to this diagnosis is that I have met many individuals who are also cancer survivors. Their strength and positive attitudes have been an inspiration to me. I have begun to do volunteer work for the American Cancer Society. I have been working on two events, the Relay for Life and the Run for Dad. The Run for Dad is designed to raise funds and awareness about prostate cancer to highlight the importance of screening and early detection.

Hope: My hope is to support the fight against prostate cancer in order to help future generations stop this disease. My husband's diagnosis of prostate cancer helped me realize what was really important in my life: the love of the individuals in my family and the satisfaction of getting up in the morning and thanking God that you are alive and well.

aggressive nature of early prostate cancer compared to late (advanced) prostate cancer, and with doctors' increasing ability to detect the disease early, and to treat the disease effectively when it is detected early. Another reason is that men who get prostate cancer tend to be older and often die of other diseases, such as heart attacks.

PROSTATE CANCER IS PRIMARILY A DISEASE OF OLDER MEN WHO DON'T DIE FROM IT

The overall lifetime risk of developing prostate cancer for a man is 1 in 6. Figure 1.2 shows the risk of developing prostate cancer as a function of age.[2] More than 15 percent of all men will be diagnosed with invasive prostate cancer. However, when the numbers are broken down by age it looks quite different.

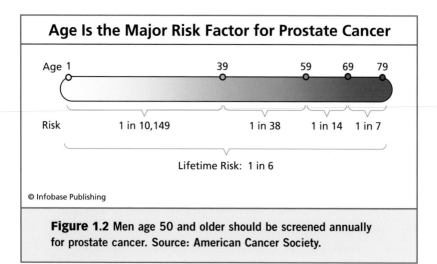

Figure 1.2 Men age 50 and older should be screened annually for prostate cancer. Source: American Cancer Society.

The risk of developing prostate cancer before the age of 40 is very low (1 in 10,149). This risk jumps to 1 in 38 for men between the ages of 40 to 59, and 1 in 7 for ages 69 to 79. Clearly the older men are, the more likely they will be diagnosed with prostate cancer. It does not mean older men will die from the disease, however. Does this mean that under-40-year-olds do not need to worry about prostate cancer? Not necessarily. There may be preventive measures that you could take to avoid developing prostate cancer later in life (see chapter 8).

Paradoxically, the younger a man is when diagnosed with prostate cancer, the more likely it is aggressive cancer that has spread to other parts of the body. One reason is that men who have prostate cancer when they are younger often have compounding genetic and possibly environmental factors that stimulate aggressive prostate cancer. Another reason is related to the age at which men are screened (see chapter 4 for more about screening). Most men are not routinely screened before age 50, or 40 for some high-risk individuals.

Table 1.2 Incidence and Mortality Rates for Prostate Cancer by Race and Ethnicity in U.S., 1998-2002*

Race/Ethnicity	Incidence	Mortality
White	169.0	27.7
African American	272.0	68.1
Asian American and Pacific Islander	101.4	12.1
American Indian and Alaska Native	50.3	18.3
Hispanic/Latino	141.9	23.0

*Rates are per 100,000 individuals.
Source: Ries LAG, Eisner MP, Kosary CL et al., eds. *SEER Cancer Statistics Review, 1975-2002*, Bethesda, Md.: National Cancer Institute. Available online. URL: http://seer.cancer.gov/csr/1975_2002/, 2005.

If a man is diagnosed with prostate cancer before 50, it is generally because he has symptoms such as bone pain, blood in his urine or semen, or painful urination. These symptoms are usually present when the cancer is advanced.

RACIAL DIFFERENCES
Despite what was said previously about prostate cancer not discriminating against any man, prostate cancer does not affect all men equally. There are clear differences in both the incidence and mortality rates among different racial groups (see Table 1.2). Prostate cancer incidence among African Americans is 1.6 times higher than for whites. In fact, African American men have the highest incidence of prostate cancer in the world. The opposite is true for Asian American and Pacific Islanders, American Indians and Alaskan Natives, and Hispanic/Latino groups, with the incidence in these groups being lower than for whites. The mortality rate in African American men is also disturbingly higher than the

incidence rates, with African American mortality 2.5 times that of whites.

The reasons for these differences between racial groups are not entirely clear. Clearly there is a genetic component to prostate cancer. This genetic contribution to prostate cancer may be associated with specific genetic differences in different racial groups. However, this has not been definitively demonstrated by the identification of specific genetic differences in different racial groups that are associated with increased (or decreased) prostate cancer risk. There is currently considerable effort to identify genetic markers for prostate cancer that can be used to identify people at high risk. Environment, diet, and access to health care also contribute to the differences among different populations

HEREDITARY PROSTATE CANCER

Prostate cancer can run in families. Often the presence of familial prostate cancer is not known by the family because information from previous generations has been lost or not discussed. Up until very recently men did not talk about prostate cancer. It was considered taboo to talk about it and this is still the case among certain groups. Men frequently do not know they have a family history of prostate cancer until they themselves are diagnosed. The following statement by Darrell Bartlett (profiled in chapter 4) describes a typical situation:

"[Just after being diagnosed] I checked in with my father. I was told there was no history of cancer in our family. Later it would turn out that my brother, my uncle [father's brother], and I were diagnosed with prostate cancer within a few months of one another. Even later, I found out that my grandfather on my father's side probably died of prostate cancer."

There is considerable evidence of hereditary prostate cancer genes both from research into inheritance patterns and from molecular genetic studies for gene identification.[2] The first gene to be identified that is mutated in some cases of hereditary prostate cancer is called HPC1 (Hereditary Prostate Cancer 1). There are now several genes that have been identified that are mutated in isolated families or groups of families with hereditary prostate cancer. None of these genes are common causes of hereditary prostate cancer, and work is ongoing

DID YOU KNOW?

Genetic causes may be responsible for 5–10 percent of prostate cancer cases. Men with a relative who has prostate cancer are at increased risk of developing prostate cancer.[3] If there is no one in your family who has had prostate cancer, then the chance of you getting diagnosed with prostate cancer is 13 percent. If your grandfather or your uncle has had prostate cancer, then the chance is 20 percent. This risk goes up to 26 percent if it is your father or your brother. Put two of these together and the chances increase dramatically. Two brothers with prostate cancer increase the chance to 65 percent. A grandfather and a father with prostate cancer and the risk is nearly 100 percent. These findings have led to scientific research on the genetics of prostate cancer. Using modern molecular genetic techniques, scientists have identified several familial prostate cancer genes. There is no one single prostate cancer gene. Some genes have been found only in a single family. Others are found in many families. There are still many families with two or more men with prostate cancer where the gene has not yet been identified. An international consortium of researchers is studying families with hereditary prostate cancer. You can find out more information at the National Cancer Institute Web site at http://www.nci.nih.gov/cancertopics/pdq/genetics/prostate/healthprofessional.

to determine the roles of these genes in sporadic (non-hereditary) prostate cancer. There are currently no commercially available genetic tests for any of the hereditary prostate cancer genes identified to date.

SPORADIC PROSTATE CANCER

Sporadic prostate cancer accounts for the vast majority (up to 90 percent) of prostate cancer cases. The mutation of genes during a person's lifetime (not inherited mutations) may account for sporadic prostate cancer. DNA mutations occur in cells in the body all of the time. These mutations may be caused by specific chemicals (carcinogens), exposure to radiation, or oxidative stress. Fortunately, your body's cells have efficient mechanisms to recognize and repair the DNA. However, some mutations slip through the repair machinery. Accumulation of mutations in certain genes may lead to prostate cancer development. Several genes have been associated with sporadic prostate cancer. **PTEN** is a gene that is mutated in 30 to 40 percent of prostate cancer cases. Animal test subjects that have had the PTEN gene mutated got prostate cancer, supporting a direct role of mutation of the PTEN gene in prostate cancer development. Other genes have also been implicated in sporadic prostate cancer development, but none with the frequency of mutations in PTEN.

ENVIRONMENT AND DIET

Environment and diet have also been suggested to play a role in differences that are observed in prostate cancer incidence among different populations.[4] The best evidence for this is from many decades of studies of Japanese immigrants to the United States. Men in Japan on a traditional Japanese diet have about 1/20th the incidence of prostate cancer of that of the general U.S. population, regardless of race. When Japanese have migrated to Hawaii, the incidence of prostate cancer in the second generation is intermediate between the incidence in

Japan and that for the mainland United States. Subsequent generations that have migrated to the mainland United States, and adopted a more Western lifestyle and diet have incidence rates that approach (but generally do not reach) the incidence in whites in the United States. How can this be explained? Geography. One could also argue that in the mainland United States, people are exposed to carcinogens and that Japan has fewer of these substances.

Several compounds have been identified that may contribute to prostate cancer development. Exposure to cadmium and pesticides are the best-characterized environmental exposures that some studies associate with increased prostate cancer. Cadmium is a common environmental toxic metal found in batteries, plastics, fish, soil, and many industrial products. Some studies, but not all, have found an increased risk of prostate cancer in men with occupational exposure to cadmium. Likewise, men who work with and around pesticides have been shown to have increased rates of prostate cancer. Chlorinated pesticides appear to be the most strongly associated. Other factors that have some weak associations include working with paints, solvents, and lubricants. For all of these environmental exposures there is still considerable controversy about the extent of the risk that they contribute to the development of prostate cancer. However, given the uncertainty, it would be wise to avoid exposure to these substances if possible.

Dietary changes are much easier to identify than carcinogen exposure in the environment. A comparison of the traditional Japanese diet to the U.S. diet (generally adopted by second- and third-generation immigrants) is relatively easy and can identify several obvious differences. The Japanese diet is much lower in calories from fat, richer in fish, and richer in soybean-derived foods, and rice. (Asian diets—which American men might do well to consider imitating—are discussed further in the "Soy Power" section of chapter 8.) Increased fat consumption from animals, decreased fish consumption (and thereby fish oils), and decreased consumption of soy products have all been associated with increased prostate cancer incidence. Other studies have also identified vitamin D (produced from exposure to the sun and also found in fish oils), selenium (a trace element), vitamin E, and lycopene (a red pigment from tomatoes) as possible protective agents against prostate cancer. However, an association is not evidence for cause and effect but is suggestive of a cause. Other studies to directly test the role of a specific dietary substance are needed to support a direct effect. Such studies can include cell culture (chapter 2 in sidebar) and animal studies (chapter 3 in sidebar), using models of prostate cancer, and human clinical trials (chapter 4 in sidebar).

With knowledge of the widespread risk of prostate cancer and basics facts about genetics, age, and race, we can explore the normal prostate in more detail, how prostate cancer is detected and treated, what controls prostate cell growth, how prostate cancer might be prevented, and how scientists study prostate cancer.

2

Prostate Anatomy and Normal Functions

To clarify the basic anatomical differences between male and female reproductive organs, Figure 2.1 compares the human male and female reproductive tracts. The prostate is a male-specific organ that contributes to the seminal fluid. The counterpart of the prostate in the female is the lower vaginal tract. Both the prostate and the vagina are derived from the same embryological structure of the fetal urogenital tract, called the urogenital sinus.[5] Under the influence of hormones these structures turn into either the vagina in females or the prostate in males (see more about hormones in chapter 6).

The prostate is a walnut-sized gland at the base of the bladder. Urine from the bladder travels through the **urethra** to the penis. The urethra goes right through the center of the prostate. This portion of the urethra is known as the prostatic urethra. The **ducts** (tubes) from the prostate empty into the prostatic urethra. The **ejaculatory ducts**, coming from the testes and seminal vesicles, also drain into the prostatic urethra at this point.[6]

The secretions of the prostate are high in sugars and proteins. The prostatic secretions are thought to be important in aiding fertilization by increasing the motility of sperm and perhaps promoting the viability of sperm after **ejaculation**. During ejaculation the contents of the ejaculatory ducts including sperm and other components of the **seminal fluid** are mixed with prostatic secretions in the prostatic urethra. The prostate gland is designed to make these secretions and deliver

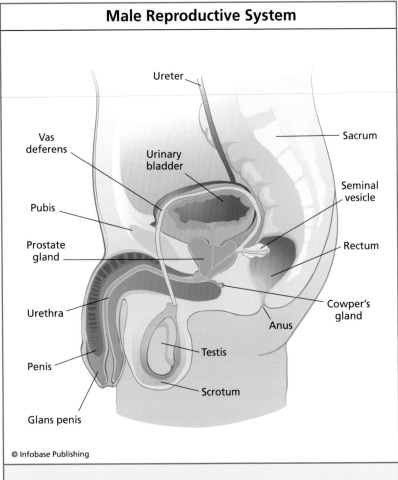

Male Reproductive System

Ureter

Vas deferens

Urinary bladder

Sacrum

Seminal vesicle

Pubis

Prostate gland

Rectum

Urethra

Cowper's gland

Anus

Penis

Testis

Glans penis

Scrotum

© Infobase Publishing

Figure 2.1a Compare the anatomy of human male and female reproductive tracts. Men have a prostate at the base of the bladder.

them as a major part of the seminal fluid (about 30 percent). The structure of the normal prostate gland is highly organized with different cell types performing specific functions. Here we will learn about the gross anatomy of the prostate and the different cell types and their organization

Female Reproductive System

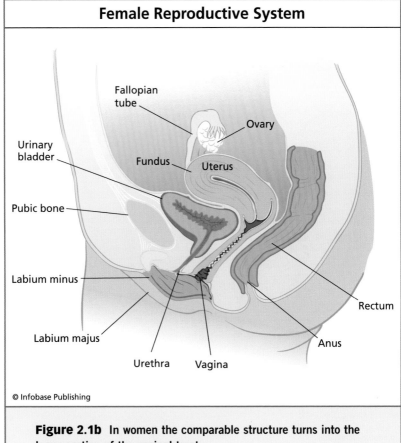

© Infobase Publishing

Figure 2.1b In women the comparable structure turns into the lower portion of the vaginal tract.

in normal prostate tissue, so that we may better understand the disorganization in the glandular structure that occurs in prostate cancer.

The prostate is an **exocrine gland**, that is, a gland that makes fluids secreted outside of the body. Other examples of exocrine glands are sweat glands, sebaceous glands (which secrete oils around hair follicles and make skin oily), salivary glands, the pancreas, and mammary glands (see Figure 2.2). All

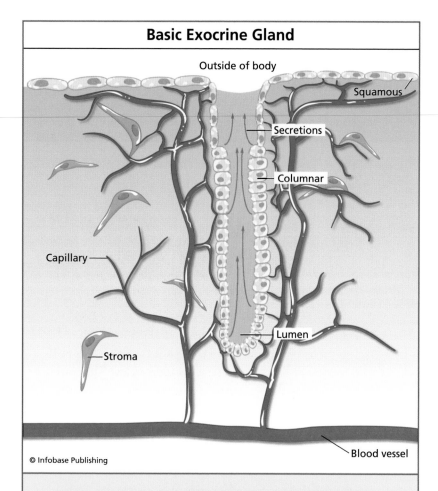

Basic Exocrine Gland

Outside of body

Squamous

Secretions

Columnar

Capillary

Stroma

Lumen

Blood vessel

© Infobase Publishing

Figure 2.2 Exocrine gland structure. Exocrine glands secrete their contents to the outside of the body. The lumen can be considered in direct contact with the outside of the body. The epithelial cells closest to the surface are usually flattened "squamous" cells. The cells that make secretions are usually tall cube-shaped cells called "columnar" cells. The material surrounding the gland (the stroma) is made of blood vessels and other cell types.

exocrine glands have a common structure of a duct lined by the cells of the **epithelium**. The opening of the duct to the outside (called the proximal portion) is lined by flattened epithelium called squamous epithelium. These proximal epithelial cells are similar to skin cells and are designed to protect the body from infection and injury. Away from the opening of the duct and farther up it, you enter the more distal portion of the duct. The epithelium in the distal portion is made up of tall columnar epithelial cells which secrete various exocrine gland products and are referred to as secretory columnar epithelial cells.

A more detailed look at the unique organization of the prostate in Figure 2.3 shows that it has a more complicated structure that resembles a branched tree. Unlike simple exocrine glands like sweat or sebaceous glands, which have a simple tube-like structure, there are multiple ducts that drain into the urethra, and each duct drains the branches of a specific region of the prostate. In between the ducts is connective tissue composed of protein fibers to hold it together, and various non-epithelial cell types that will be discussed below. The connective tissue is called the **stroma** and it's made up of stromal cells. Thus the two main classes of cell types in the prostate are the epithelial cells and the stromal cells.

There are different zones of the prostate that are drained by specific ducts and have unique features distinguishing them from other zones, including being drained by specific ducts.[7] These different zones have susceptibilities to three main prostatic diseases[8]: the central zone, which is at the top of the prostate and is very resistant to BPH and prostate cancer; the transition zone, toward the front of the prostate and very prone to BPH (about 10–15 percent of prostate cancer cases also occurs in this zone); and the peripheral zone, at the back and to the sides of the prostate, which is very susceptible to cancer (85–90 percent of cases). The different locations are used in diagnosing prostate cancer and will be discussed in chapter 4.

Zonal Anatomy of Prostate (Side View)

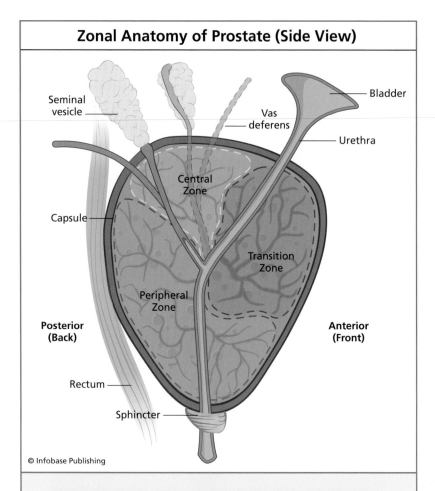

Seminal vesicle

Vas deferens

Bladder

Urethra

Central Zone

Capsule

Transition Zone

Peripheral Zone

Posterior (Back)

Anterior (Front)

Rectum

Sphincter

© Infobase Publishing

Figure 2.3 Zonal anatomy of the prostate. The human prostate is composed of "zones" of exocrine glandular tissue with the ducts emptying into the prostatic urethra. The central zone (yellow) is at the top of the prostate near the bladder and is resistant to both BPH and prostate cancer. The ejaculatory ducts pass through the central zone to the urethra. The transition zone (pink) surrounds the portion of the urethra closest to the bladder and is the site of BPH and some cancer. The peripheral zone (blue) is located at the posterior side of the prostate closest to the rectum and is highly susceptible to cancer.

These differences also help explain the side effects of BPH, which is an enlargement of the prostate. You can see from Figure 2.3 that the prostatic urethra is surrounded by the transition zone. When the BPH occurs in this area it compresses the urethra and makes it difficult to urinate. The most common symptom of BPH is frequency of urination, especially at night.

Histology is the study of tissue organization at the cellular level. A **pathologist** is a medical doctor who studies diseases by observing changes in the structure of tissue. In order to understand the changes in histology associated with a disease, also

USE OF CELL CULTURE TO STUDY PROSTATE CANCER

Prostate cancer researchers often use isolated cells grown in the laboratory to study different aspects of prostate biology. The growth of cells in the laboratory outside of an animal is called cell culture. Techniques have been developed to grow human cells fresh from a surgical sample. A researcher can grow both prostate cancer cells and the normal cells from the same prostate. This allows the researcher to compare the different responses of the normal and cancerous prostatic cells to a given experiment. Generally the normal cells grown from a fresh sample have a limited life span from a few weeks to a few months. Some prostate cancer cell lines have been developed. A cancer cell line is a strain of cancer cells that can grow indefinitely. The advantage of these cell lines is that they can be used by several laboratories all over the world so results can be compared. These cell lines can also be grown in animals to test experimental therapies (see Did You Know? box in chapter 3). Prostate cells are used for the early studies to determine the effects of a potential drug or treatment on cell growth and cell death.

called the pathology of a disease, one needs to understand the basic histological organization of healthy tissue.[9] As mentioned above, the prostate is an exocrine gland that contains columnar epithelium that lines a series of branching ducts. A closer examination at the histological level reveals multiple cell types organized into a very specific pattern. Figure 2.4 is a photomicrograph (a picture taken through a microscope) of a section from a human prostate. This section shows the normal organization of the prostate in the peripheral zone (see Figure 2.3). The gland contains a **lumen**, which is the open space of the duct that accepts the prostatic secretions. Figure 2.5 is a schematic drawing of a normal prostate gland showing the different cell types. As discussed before, the major cell types in the normal prostate are the epithelial cells, which make up the prostatic ducts and the stromal cells. Four major types of epithelial cells exist in the ducts: secretory columnar epithelial cells, basal epithelial cells, neuroendocrine cells, and stem cells. Stromal cells consist of smooth muscle fibroblasts and their precursors, endothelial cells that comprise the blood vessels, and miscellaneous immune cells.

LUMINAL CELLS

Lining the lumen is a tube of secretory columnar epithelial cells, also known as **luminal epithelial cells**. A major product of the luminal epithelial cells is a protein known as **prostate specific antigen (PSA)**. No other cell in the male body normally produces significant amounts of PSA. PSA is made in very small amounts in breast epithelial cells, salivary epithelial cells, and some non-prostate tumor cells. Because PSA is concentrated most in prostate cells, it can be used as a marker for prostate cells. (The use of PSA as a marker for prostate cancer will be discussed in chapter 4.) PSA is a **proteolytic enzyme**, that is, an enzyme that cuts up other proteins. Prostate researchers think that the normal role of PSA is to cleave a protein called

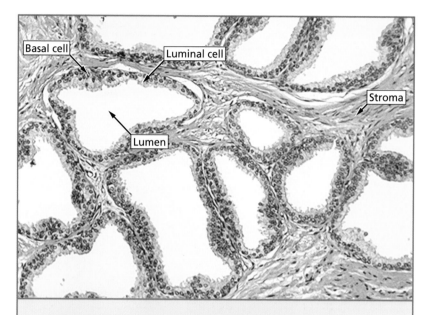

Figure 2.4 Histology of the normal prostate. A section of prostate gland magnified 55 times. Note that all of the glands are surrounded by a more or less continuous layer of basal cells and the glands are separated by stroma. © Carolina Biological Supply Company/Phototake

seminogellin, which is made by the seminal vesicles. Seminogellin is a very large protein that prevents the final maturation of sperm. Mature sperm swims by beating its flagellum (tail). Before it is mature it cannot move its flagellum. Seminogellin is also sometimes called motility inhibitory factor because it inhibits the flagellum of the sperm from moving. During ejaculation the contents of the prostate mix with the contents of the seminal vesicles and ejaculatory ducts. This mixing allows the contact of PSA with the seminogellin. The proteolytic action of PSA cleaves seminogellin into smaller pieces, preventing seminogellin from inhibiting sperm motility and allowing the sperm to fully mature and be ready for fertilization.

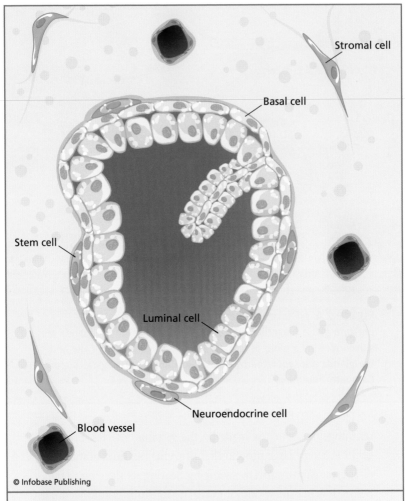

Figure 2.5 Cell types in the prostate. This figure shows a drawing of an idealized normal prostate gland with the different cell types. Compare this schematic of the different types of cells in the prostate with Figure 2.4.

BASAL CELLS

The **basal** epithelial cells surround the luminal cells and act as a physical barrier between the luminal cells and the surrounding stroma. Because the lumens of the prostate are

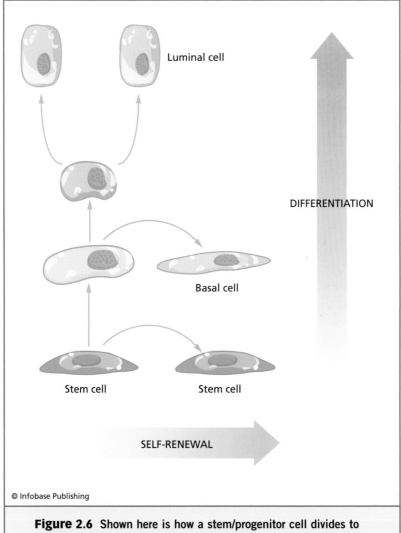

Figure 2.6 Shown here is how a stem/progenitor cell divides to regenerate itself (self-renewal) and to differentiate into the basal and luminal cells.

essentially contiguous with the outside of the body (as are all exocrine glands), they are potential sites for entry of disease pathogens such as bacteria, fungi, or viruses. The basal cells act as a barrier to pathogen entry into the rest of the body.

The basal cells secrete a complex protein-rich substance at the interface with the surrounding stroma (the side away from the lumen, see figures 2.5 and 3.1). This protein-rich substance is known as the basal lamina, or basement membrane. For a pathogen to enter the body it must penetrate through the luminal layer, the basal layer, and then the basal lamina before it can have access to the local blood supply and thereby entry into the rest of the body (see figure 2.5). The basal cells respond directly to hormonal signals from the

LINUS PAULING

Born: February 28, 1901, Portland, Oregon
Died: Prostate cancer, August 19, 1994, Big Sur, California
Linus Pauling was diagnosed with prostate cancer in 1991 at 90 years old. He was too old and the cancer too advanced for surgery. He underwent external beam irradiation in 1992. He died of metastatic prostate cancer at the age of 93 at his ranch in the coastal California community of Big Sur.

Considered by many to be the most influential scientist of the twentieth century next to Albert Einstein, Linus Pauling is the only person to win two unshared Nobel prizes[10], one in chemistry in 1954 for his work in quantum mechanics and the nature of chemical bonds, and one for peace in 1962 for his active protests against nuclear proliferation and atmospheric testing of nuclear bombs. He wrote more than 1,000 articles and books. He solved the genetic basis of sickle cell anemia by studying hemoglobin protein structure. He galvanized the scientific community and the world with his protests against atmospheric nuclear testing. He is perhaps best known for his promotion of the health benefits of vitamin C. He was never shy of controversy, from his early work on the blood. They also exert local growth control on the luminal epithelial cells and surrounding stromal cells through various secreted signals.

NEUROENDOCRINE CELLS

Located within the basal layer is also a rare population of specialized cells called **neuroendocrine cells**. These cells have features of neuronal cells and they make signaling molecules that may help control prostate growth and differentiation. The

nature of the chemical bond and his peace activism, to his proposition that mega-doses of vitamin C would prevent the common cold and numerous other chronic illnesses, including cancer.

Figure 2.7 Linus Pauling. © AP Images

origin of these cells and their exact role in the prostate is still a subject of debate.

STEM CELLS

Adult **stem/progenitor cells** are located in nearly every tissue in the body. These cells act as a reserve for regenerating the tissue after injury and for regenerating cells in the tissue that die due to normal aging. There are two characteristics that are used to define adult stem cells: the ability for self-renewal and the ability to change into multiple cell types. This process of **differentiation** is often referred to as multilineage differentiation. These definitions refer to the fate of the cell after a cell divides.

Cell division is the process of a cell making two copies of itself. The process of cell division is beyond the scope if this book, but can be found in biology textbooks.[10] In cell division, which is a kind of self-renewal, the cell division results in the generation of new stem cells. In multilineage differentiation the stem cells change into different cell types that make up the tissue. Recent studies suggest that the adult prostate contains stem cells. These prostatic stem cells are thought to be located within the basal layer of the prostate. Research suggests that the stem cells are a rare cell (1/100) in the basal layer that serves as a reservoir of undifferentiated cells. Figure 2.6 shows a diagram of the potential role of prostate stem cells in generating the other prostate epithelial cells. Under appropriate signals from the surrounding tissue, stem cells are induced to undergo asymmetric (unequal) cell divisions to repopulate the different cell types within the prostate gland. In other words, one daughter cell becomes another stem cell and the other daughter cell goes on to further divisions that lead to the differentiated basal, luminal, and perhaps neuroendocrine cells of the mature prostate gland. Many researchers now believe that these cells have features similar to cancer cells, suggesting that they may give rise to prostate cancer.

After discussing the cytological and histological features of the normal prostate, we can describe what happens to these features in prostate cancer.

3

Prostate Cancer Pathology and Grading

"It was May and we had been planning a trip to Victoria, B.C. The pathology report was not due back for several days. The urologist urged us to take our trip as planned. At the world-famous Butchart Gardens north of Victoria there is a statue of a bronze boar. A sign said KISS THE BOAR'S SNOUT AND YOUR EVERY WISH WILL COME TRUE. I kissed the boar's snout at least six times and wished for a 'No Cancer' pathology report on my return. The report showed I had a Gleason 7, prostate cancer. I will never kiss another pig."

—Norton Ernest, Chico, CA (see Norton's profile in chapter 6)

In this chapter we will discuss the histological (tissue) changes that occur in the prostate and how doctors use these changes to determine the aggressiveness of the cancer. The determination is important because the doctor and the patient use this information to decide how various therapies may be able to treat the cancer. It can also be used after the patient has been treated—by surgery, for example—to determine the likelihood that he has been cured. This assessment of the future health of the patient is known as the **prognosis**.

The histological features of the normal prostate were discussed in the previous chapter. There are two main epithelial cell types: a single layer of flattened basal cells and a single layer of secretory columnar luminal cells. During the development of prostate cancer, the normal prostate structure is altered, leading to a more aggressive disease. The main changes result in a breakdown of the basal cell barrier between the prostatic duct and the surrounding stroma. These breakdowns lead to invasion of luminal cells into the surrounding stroma, which can eventually lead to migration of these cells into the rest of the body using the nervous or circulatory systems.

PROSTATIC INTRAEPITHELIAL NEOPLASIA— A PRECURSOR TO PROSTATE CANCER

The piling up of luminal cells in the prostate is called **prostatic intraepithelial neoplasia** (**PIN**). PIN is now thought to be a precursor to prostate cancer. (A cartoon model of the changes that occur in the structure of the prostate is shown in Figure 3.1.) PIN is usually segregated into low grade and high grade, depending on how closely it resembles true prostate cancer.[11] Keep in mind that PIN retains a basal cell layer, distinguishing PIN from prostate cancer, which lacks a basal layer. Notice in figure 3.1 that the normal luminal cells are

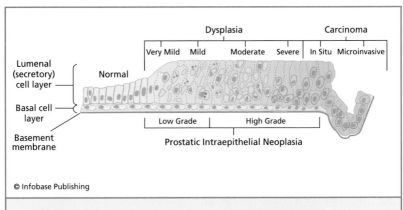

© Infobase Publishing

Figure 3.1 Cellular changes in prostatic intraepithelial neoplasia. The progressive changes in the structure of the gland is seen going from left (normal) to right (microinvasive carcinoma). Note that PIN is always associated with an intact basal cell layer. Adapted from Bostwick, D.G., and M.K. Brawer "Prostatic intraepithelial neoplasia and early invasion in prostate cancer" *Cancer*, 59 (1987): 788–794.

very similar to one another in size, shape, and the location of the nucleus (the round circle within the cells) toward the basal layer.[12] In low-grade PIN the luminal cells become less uniform; the nuclei are no longer located solely at the basal layer, becoming enlarged and containing enlarged dark spots referred to as nucleoli. The cells appear to be piled on top of each other. In high-grade PIN these characteristics become more pronounced, the nuclei become very large and the nucleoli are very prominent, and the basal layer begins to have small gaps. In early prostate cancer (**carcinoma**), there is an additional loss of the complete basal layer.

USE OF ANIMALS TO STUDY PROSTATE CANCER

Animal research has played an essential role in the study of prostate cancer. The pioneering work of Charles B. Huggins on the hormonal treatment of prostate cancer was discovered in dogs (see sidebar in chapter 6). Dogs are only rarely used in prostate cancer research today; more common laboratory test animals are rats and mice. There are now multiple models of prostate cancer both in rats and mice. These rodent models are routinely used for drugs for the treatment of prostate cancer prior to their entry into a clinical trial (see sidebar in chapter 4). With advances in genetic engineering, mice get prostate cancer that mimics human prostate cancer. This includes the development of precancerous lesions that look like prostatic intraepithelial neoplasia (PIN) as well as invasive cancer and prostate cancer metastases, or the spread of cancer to other parts of the body (see chapter 7). These animal models have been used extensively to identify new therapeutic targets for treatment as well as for studying the effects of preventive agents (see chapter 8).

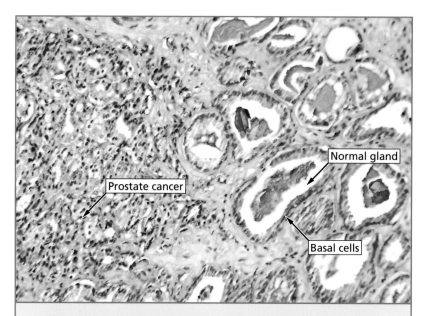

Figure 3.2 Histology of prostate cancer. Prostate cancer lacks a basal layer and has smaller gland size. This section from a human prostate is magnified 300 times. On the right is somewhat normal tissue with moderately differentiated cancer. The left shows highly undifferentiated prostate cancer. Note the more normal glands have a basal layer. Photo © National Cancer Institute

THE GLEASON GRADING SYSTEM

One of the defining attributes of prostate cancer that distinguishes it from PIN and normal prostate glands is the loss of a basal layer of cells. Figure 3.2 shows an example of this in a prostate sample. However, loss of the basal layer is not the end of the process of changes in the prostate that lead to aggressive prostate cancer. Just as with PIN, in which there are low-grade and high-grade classifications of aggressiveness, there are specific changes that occur in the prostate that have been associated with more or less aggressive disease. There are several systems that have been developed to classify these changes and correlate them with patient survival and response to therapy.

The system that is used throughout the world is the Gleason grading system developed by Donald Gleason in the 1960s.[13,14] Gleason developed a standardized system of grading histological changes in prostate glandular structure that could be used to predict prostatic disease progression. Figure 3.3 shows a figure that Gleason published in 1966 that is still used by pathologists to grade prostate cancer with the Gleason system. The figure is meant to represent the appearance of the prostate glandular morphology at low magnification in a microscope. To understand this diagram, look at the label with the number 1. Imagine that each circle represents the lumen of a duct or gland. Gleason noticed that as the prostate cancer gets more aggressive the glandular structure gets less uniform and more disorganized. This organization is often referred to as the degree of differentiation. The more organized (grade 1), the more differentiated. The less organized (grade 5), the less differentiated, and the more aggressive the cancer. From 1 to 5, each number is assigned an increasing **Gleason grade**. There are a variety of glandular types that can be classified as belonging to each specific grade. In general, as the Gleason grade increases, the size and shape of the glands become less uniform. In very advanced cancer, Gleason grade 4 or 5, the glands become very tiny, or there is no glandular structure at all.

THE GLEASON SCORE

At the beginning of this chapter, Norton Ernest is quoted as saying that he had a Gleason 7 cancer. Although the Gleason grades run between 1 and 5, the Gleason grading system is augmented by Gleason's scoring system. In many prostate cancer specimens there is not just one type of glandular structure or Gleason grade. There is often a combination of types of glandular structures with varying degrees of differentiation and Gleason grades. Donald Gleason recognized this variation and developed a scoring system. In a given prostate sample he assigned a number to the most common pattern and a second number to the next most common pattern. Both grades are based on the Gleason grading system shown in Figure 3.3. The two numbers are added together to obtain the **Gleason score**. The lowest Gleason score is 2 (1+1) and the highest is 10 (5+5). In practice it is rare for a pathologist to grade a cancer 1 or 2. Gleason grades 3, 4, and 5 are much more common. Therefore, the Gleason 7 score Norton Ernest described at the chapter opening was either Gleason grades 3+4 cancer or 5+2.

HOW IS THE GLEASON GRADING SYSTEM USED?

Some cancers are more aggressive—that is, more deadly—than others. One of the great challenges of the pathologist is to predict the cancer aggressiveness. Many men who are diagnosed with prostate cancer elect to be treated with surgery to remove the prostate. This surgery is called **prostatectomy** and is discussed in more detail in chapter 5. The idea behind this surgery is that if the cancer has not spread from the prostate, then the man will be cured. However, not all men are cured by radical prostatectomy when the prostate is removed after the cancer has already spread. These men will be diagnosed with metastatic prostate cancer—cancer that has spread to other places in the body. It is this **metastasis** to other organs in the body that can kill a person. Gleason thought that his grading system might help in establishing the prognosis of who would be likely to already have metastatic prostate cancer. The test of time has shown this to be true: The higher the Gleason score, the more aggressive the disease is likely to be.

In Table 3.1 progression-free risk refers to the short- and long-term expectations (in percentages) of men who have no detectable symptoms of prostate cancer and of men with Gleason scores of 8–9. You can see that men whose Gleason scores are between 2–4 are 100 percent disease-free at five years and 95.6 percent disease-free at 10 years. At the other extreme, of men whose Gleason scores are 8–9, only 59.1 percent are disease-free at five years and 34.9 percent at 10 years. The Gleason

Prostatic Adenocarcinoma
(Histologic Grades)

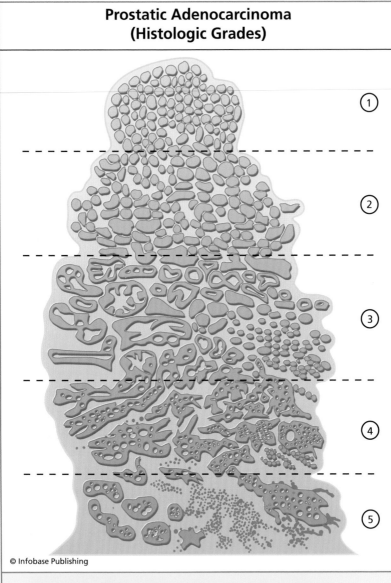

© Infobase Publishing

Figure 3.3 Gleason Grading System. As prostate cancer becomes more aggressive, the glands become less organized, with smaller and more variable lumen sizes. Highly aggressive cancer can have obvious lumens. Each panel from top to bottom represents an increasing Gleason grade.

Table 3.1 Gleason Score and Progression-free Risk*

Gleason score at Surgery	Progression-free risk (in percentages)	
	5 Years from Diagnosis	10 Years from Diagnosis
2–4	100	95.6
5–6	96.9	81.9
7	76.9	51.4
8–9	59.1	34.9

* *Source*: Modified from Epstein, J.I. "Pathologic Features that Predict Progression of Disease Following Radical Prostatectomy," in eds. Foster, C.S., and D.G. Bostwick, *Pathology of the Prostate*. Philadelphia, Pa.: W.B. Saunders Company, 1998, pp. 228-244

score is only one measure that is used to predict disease-free survival. Other considerations used to predict disease-free survival include tumor volume, cancer in lymph nodes, and invasion into the prostate capsule. All of these are measures of evidence of metastasis. Doctors use all of these considerations when determining the risk that a man will have metastatic prostate cancer. Notice that not all men with Gleason 8–9 have recurrent prostate cancer. Note the use of the word *risk* above: The Gleason grading system is a predictive tool that gives a probability that someone will **relapse** (the cancer will recur). It is not an absolute that someone with a Gleason 9 will have metastatic prostate cancer. The Gleason score can help determine who should be more closely watched for **disease progression**, or who might benefit more from treatment before cancer recurs.

After this introduction to the pathology of prostate cancer and the use of the Gleason grading system for predictions, the next chapter will discuss how prostate cancer is detected.

KATIE RUFF, GRADUATE STUDENT, COLORADO STATE UNIVERSITY

During my freshman year of college, about 1,500 miles away from home, my father called to tell me something I never expected to hear at the age of 19. He had prostate cancer. Of course I was upset; it was my *father* who has cancer. I was told that I did not need to worry—they got all of the cancer and he would not need further treatment. When I returned home for the summer I saw that my father no longer had hair on his chest and was talking about hormone therapy. I knew that things were more serious than I had been told several months ago. After reading pathology reports, I looked up everything I could about prostate cancer so I could understand the details of my dad's continuous and possible future treatments for my own peace of mind and to attempt to offer support to my parents when they had to make treatment decisions.

Now I am in graduate school in Colorado doing cancer research, which I had wanted to do even before my father was diagnosed with cancer. I want to make whatever contribution I can in the field of cancer research, wherever I may live. Knowing that my dad has not lost his spirit and will never give up, I am able to go on with my life, doing what makes me happy.

If you have a parent battling cancer, try not to put your life on hold or do just what you think you should do for your family. I believe that it is best to know the details involved with a parent's cancer, so do not be afraid to ask questions and remember that it is normal to be scared at times. No one has control of the situation, so just do the best you can to help your family and have faith that everything will work out, whatever the outcome. The more active and informed you are, the better you will feel and the more help you will be to your family.

4

Prostate Cancer Screening and Diagnosis

"I was diagnosed in October 2000, just a few days prior to my 49th birthday. Prostate cancer was detected as part of my annual physical. The doctor felt a hardness on the prostate that he did not like, but he was sure 'it was nothing' because of my age. The PSA test came back at 8.0, which was high, but again 'probably nothing.' A prostate biopsy was scheduled. The biopsy was positive for prostate cancer and indicated a very large tumor encompassing both lobes of the prostate. The grading indicated an aggressive tumor, Gleason 4+4."?

—Darrell Bartlett (see Darrell's profile, this chapter)

Darrell Bartlett's discovery that he had prostate cancer is an example of the most common methods involved in the detection of prostate cancer. These processes include a routine annual physical examination, which can include a prostate examination (digital rectal examination) and a blood test (PSA test). These two screening strategies are used to identify men who should be evaluated further. If either of these test results is abnormal, then a sample of the prostate (biopsy) will be taken to look at the pathology and assign a Gleason grade. Only a prostate biopsy can definitively diagnose prostate cancer. Some men are diagnosed after they come to the doctor complaining of bloody urine, painful urination, or sometimes bone pain.

DIGITAL RECTAL EXAMINATION

The prostate gland is located just below the bladder and the urethra goes through the prostate. As you can see in Figure 2.1, the prostate is also located just in front of the rectum. The orientation of the prostate is such that its peripheral zone is located closest to the rectum, and approximately 75–80 percent of prostate cancers are located in the peripheral zone of the prostate. This allows a doctor to feel the prostate to identify any areas of abnormality. This procedure is called a **digital rectal examination (DRE).** To perform a DRE, the doctor uses a gloved index or middle finger to feel the prostate through the rectal wall. With little effort, an experienced physician can determine the size and hardness of the prostate. A normal, healthy prostate will be about the size of a walnut and uniformly soft and pliable. Areas of prostate cancer will often feel harder than the surrounding normal area. This hardened area can be as little as the size of a pea (or smaller) and sometimes much bigger, and is often called a **nodule**. The presence of a hardened nodule is cause for suspicion of prostate cancer and grounds for further testing. The prostate can also be larger than a normal-sized prostate, but this is more often due to BPH rather than prostate cancer. The presence of a large prostate without hardened areas is not usually sufficient cause for a needle biopsy, but it may prompt the doctor to order a PSA blood test.

Use of the DRE as a primary screen for prostate cancer is very effective as the first clue to the doctor that a man has a prostate problem. One problem with the DRE is that it is based on the doctor's ability to feel differences. It is subject to the doctor's interpretation, which means the test is subjective. If the cancer is not particularly hard or if it is located away from the rectal surface of the prostate, then the doctor might miss the cancer. It is also true that some doctors have a better ability to feel areas of cancer than do others. A **urologist** is a doctor who treats the urogenital tract, which includes the prostate. A urologist may perform hundreds of DREs in a month, or even more if the urologist is involved in large-scale screening clinics. A family physician may perform only a few a month. It therefore makes sense that the urologist is likely to be more sensitive to what a normal prostate feels like

WHAT IS A CLINICAL TRIAL?

A clinical trial is designed to test a new treatment's effect on a specific disease in humans. The treatment can be a new prevention strategy, a new surgical method, or a new drug. Clinical trials are designed to test a hypothesis that the new treatment will have a certain effect on the disease (see sidebar in chapter 7). Extensive preclinical testing is done before conducting a clinical trial in humans. These preclinical tests will often include laboratory studies in animal and human cell culture (see sidebar in chapter 2) and in animal models of the disease (see sidebar in chapter 3).

There are three phases of clinical trials.

Phase I trials: These first human studies are designed to test safety and methods of administration. Usually only a few people are enrolled in a phase I trial.

Phase II trials: A phase II trial continues to test the safety of the drug, and begins to evaluate how well the new drug works. Phase II studies usually focus on a particular type of cancer.

Phase III trials: These studies test a new drug, a new combination of drugs, or a new surgical procedure in comparison to the current standard. A participant will usually be assigned to the standard therapy or to the new therapy at random (a process called randomization). Phase III trials often enroll large numbers of people and may be conducted at many doctors' offices, clinics, and cancer centers nationwide. A phase III trial is designed to test a hypothesis so that definite conclusions can be drawn.

Information about clinical trials for cancer can be found at www.cancer.gov/clinicaltrials.

versus what a prostate cancer nodule feels like. It may also be helpful to have the same doctor perform the DRE each year, so that he or she is familiar with what the prostate felt like at the last examination.

The DRE screening test does not provide a diagnosis for prostate cancer—this can only come from looking at the pathology of the prostate, usually from a sample taken by needle biopsy—but it has the major advantage of being quick, easy, and inexpensive.

THE PSA TEST

The Prostate specific antigen (PSA) is a protein that is made almost exclusively by the prostate and is part of the normal functions of the prostate. PSA was discovered in the late 1960s and was first used in forensic analysis to test for semen at crime scenes. However, since the 1980s, its detection in blood has been developed into the most widespread cancer screening test in use today. In the normal prostate, PSA is secreted into the lumen. The blood vessels in the prostate are located in the stroma, which is physically separated from the prostate lumens by the basal cells and the basement membrane. Because of this physical separation, very little PSA is found in the blood of men without prostate cancer. More important, PSA is made by prostate cancer cells. In many men with prostate cancer, the blood levels of PSA increase. In chapter 3 we saw that there is a breakdown or loss of the basal layer and invasion of the prostate cancer cells into the **stroma**. This invasion results in closer association of the cancer cells with the blood vessels, allowing PSA levels to increase in the blood.

A blood test can be used to measure accurate levels of PSA. Several companies market PSA screening tests. These tests all rely on the use of **antibodies** that bind specifically to the PSA protein. Antibodies are proteins that are normally made by the immune system to fight off infections, and every antibody has a unique amino acid sequence that is designed to recognize and

Table 4.1 Adjusted PSA Reference Ranges

Age	Asian	Black	White
40-49	0-2.0	0-2.0	0-2.5
50-59	0-3.0	0-4.0	0-3.5
60-69	0-4.0	0-4.5	0-4.5
70-79	0-5.0	0-5.5	0-6.5

Source: Oesterling, J.E., and M.A. Moyad, *The ABCs of Prostate Cancer: The Book that Could Save Your Life*. Lantham, Md.: Madison Books, 1997. Reprinted by permission.

bind to other molecules. The PSA test measures the amount of protein in a given volume of blood. The units are measured by the metric system. The protein is measured in mass as nanograms. One nanogram (ng) is one one-billionth of a gram, or 10^{-9} grams. The blood is measured in milliliters. One milliliter (ml) is one one-thousandth of a liter, or 10^{-3} liters.

The amount of PSA in the blood of a man younger than 40 years old who has no prostatic disease is usually below 1 ng/ml, and often it is undetectable by the most sensitive **assays**. PSA values increase in men as they get older, even in the absence of prostate cancer. This normal increase is due primarily to an increase in prostate volume (size) due to BPH. Because there is some amount of PSA in the blood that is not related to prostate cancer, certain cutoff values are used to determine the risk of prostate cancer. If a man's PSA is below a certain level, then there is little or no suspicion of prostate cancer (as long as there are no other suspicious findings). Most doctors agree that blood PSA levels below 4 ng/ml are normal. If the blood PSA level is above 4 ng/ml, however, then this suggests that further tests should be done. Because PSA levels tend to increase as a man gets older, some doctors use age-adjusted PSA levels. There are also racial differences in

PSA. Table 4.1 has a sampling of age- and race-adjusted PSA cutoff values. (Note, however, that not everyone agrees with the use of adjusted PSA values.)

The PSA test, like the DRE, is used in screening to identify men who should be evaluated further by needle biopsy. PSA is specific for prostate cells, but not prostate cancer cells. As has already been discussed, the normal prostatic luminal cells make PSA and secrete it into the lumen. The amount of PSA made by a prostate is related to the amount of prostate tissue, normal or diseased. BPH is an enlargement of the prostate that can contribute to the amount of PSA in the blood. Prostatitis can also increase the blood levels of PSA. These contributions to blood PSA levels from other prostatic diseases greatly complicate the use of the PSA test for predicting the presence of prostate cancer. There is a gray zone of PSA between the range of 4–10 ng/ml where the contributions from BPH and prostatitis cannot be distinguished from the contribution from prostate cancer. PSA values above 10 ng/ml almost always indicate the presence of prostate cancer. In advanced prostate cancer PSA levels above 1000 ng/ml are not unusual.

The PSA blood test is simple, accurate, and inexpensive. Millions of men are screened annually. A major advantage of the PSA test is that it is highly reproducible and is not subject to interpretation like the DRE. It is a quantitative measure with a defined numerical value. There are two major disadvantages to the test, however: false positives and false negatives. The lack of prostate cancer specificity and the contributions of BPH, and prostatitis, affect blood levels of PSA. This lack of specificity can result in high PSA levels that suggest **false positives** and cause unnecessary biopsies. The other disadvantage is the potential for **false negatives**, that is, the danger of missing actual prostate cancer because of a low blood PSA level. Not all prostate cancers make PSA. About 10 percent of prostate cancers are what are called neuroendocrine tumors, which generally do not make significant amounts of PSA but are often deadly. Other prostate cancers might not result in an increase in blood PSA despite their ability to make PSA. The impact of these false negatives should not be underestimated. The PSA test is not perfect. There are many laboratories working to develop a better test for prostate cancer screening.

TRANSRECTAL ULTRASOUND-GUIDED PROSTATE NEEDLE BIOPSY

If either the DRE or the PSA test are abnormal, then the doctor usually will recommend that a biopsy be taken. A **biopsy** is a sample of tissue that is then examined under the microscope by a pathologist. The sample is taken with a fine needle that is inserted through the rectal wall into the prostate to remove a core (see Figure 4.1). To guide the needle the doctor will use an ultrasound probe. Ultrasound uses sound waves to make images of the tissue. To obtain an image of the prostate, an ultrasound probe with an attached needle is inserted into the rectum. The needle is guided to the desired location and the needle is inserted into the prostate to remove a core. The doctor will usually take needle cores from at least six different locations in the prostate. Taking six cores allows for a good sampling of the prostate.

The needle cores removed from the prostate are immediately sent to the pathologist who will determine whether cancer is present or not. Figure 4.1 shows some examples of histology from prostate needle biopsies. The pathologist will also look for PIN, the precursor to cancer (see chapter 3). If cancer is present, the Gleason score will be determined. If there is high-grade PIN but no cancer, the doctor will often recommend that another biopsy be taken about a month later. About half of men who have high-grade PIN but no cancer in the first biopsy are found to have cancer in the second biopsy.

If no cancer is found in the biopsy, nothing more is done. The man will come back the next year for a DRE and another

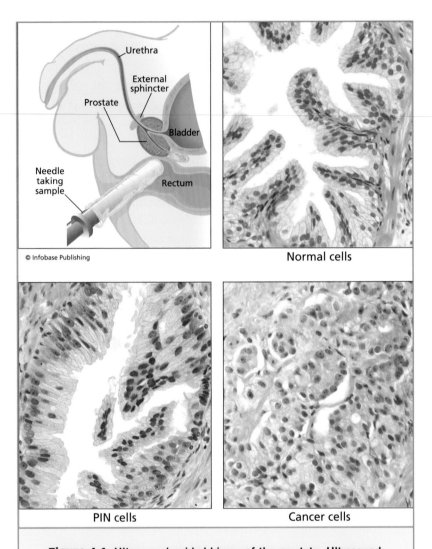

Normal cells

PIN cells

Cancer cells

Figure 4.1 Ultrasound guided biopsy of the prostate. Ultrasound is used to guide the needle to the proper location in the prostate. There are usually six and sometimes more biopsies taken from different locations.The photos show examples of normal, PIN, and cancer cells. Photos courtesy Dharam M. Ramnani, M.D./www.WebPathology.com

Table 4.2 **Staging of Prostate Cancer***

Clinical Findings	American (ABC)	TNM
Nonpalpable Cancer	A (1,2)	T1 (a,b)
detected by biopsy	B0	T1c
Palpable Cancer		
≤ half of one lobe	B1	T2a
> half of one lobe, but not both lobes	B1	T2b
both lobes	B2	T2c
Cancer with Local Extraprostatic Invasion		
one side	C1	T3a
both sides	C1	T3b
seminal vesicle invasion	C2	T3c
invasion of bladder, rectum, sphincter	C2	T4a
invasion of pelvic wall	C2	T4b
Metastatic Cancer		
lymph node invasion	D1	N (1,2,3)
distant metastases	D3	M1 (a,b,c)

* *Source*: Adapted from Foster, C.S., and D.G. Bostwick, *Pathology of the Prostate*. Philadelphia: W.B. Saunders, 1998.

PSA test. If the results are still abnormal the next year, and especially if the test results are worse, then another biopsy will be performed at that time.

STAGING THE CANCER

If cancer is found, then the course of action for treatment depends on the determination of how aggressive the cancer is. **Staging** refers to the process of determining the degree that the prostate cancer has spread through the prostate gland and to other parts of the body. There are two main systems currently used to determine the stage of cancer, the American (ABCD

DARRELL BARTLETT

Born: October 1951

Diagnosed in October 2000, just a few days prior to his forty-ninth birthday. Prostate cancer was detected as part of his annual physical; the doctor felt a hardness on the prostate that he did not like, but he was not too worried yet because of Darrell's relative youth. The PSA test came back at 8.0, which was high, so the doctor scheduled a biopsy. The biopsy was positive and indicated a very large tumor encompassing both lobes of the prostate. The grading, Gleason 4+4, indicated an aggressive tumor, and the Gleason score was 8.

While all other tests were negative, because of his age, high Gleason rating, and the size of the tumor, Darrell decided to treat it aggressively. At the time, all of the data indicated that surgery was not helpful for a tumor that likely had already grown beyond the prostate. Data from new studies now indicate this may not be true. Also, there was little good data at the time about hormone therapy.

Darrell says, "It was only then, after all of the research, understanding my cancer, and finally determining my treatment, that I was ready to start telling family and friends. Telling my daughters was the hardest thing; I felt so helpless to ease their fear."

Darrell started hormone ablation therapy, which lasted for 15 months. After three months, his PSA had dropped to an undetectable level. So it was time to begin five weeks of external beam radiation, which was expanded to treat the prostate as well as surrounding area, including lymph nodes and seminal vesicles. Two weeks after completing external beam radiation, he underwent brachytherapy with 51 seeds of radioactive palladium inserted into his prostate. (Technical terms are explained near the beginning of the following chapter and in the Glossary at the back of the book.)

Darrell is now 53, and works at California State University– Chico, where he supports Macintosh computers and repairs laser printers. He received his training in electronics and computers in

Figure 4.2 Darrell Bartlett. Courtesy the Bartlett family

the U.S. Navy and served aboard nuclear submarines. He joined the Navy in 1969, when he was just 17 years old. After serving in the Navy and graduating from University of California, Santa Cruz, he married his sweetheart, and had three children. He has been at CSU–Chico for more than 23 years. He loves to hike, garden, read, and travel.

Darrell says, "I am doing fine now, with almost no collateral damage from my treatments. I feel very fortunate. I have become active in the American Cancer Society Man to Man program where I enjoy learning from other survivors, and being a good listener. I serve on the survivor committee for our local American Cancer Society Relay for Life."

Darrell's advice to others: "Live well! By that I mean really live fully. Play hard, have adventures and experiences that keep you strong and vital. Eat well, and especially enjoy a large variety of foods. Eat more fruits and vegetables than meat. But enjoy what you eat. Love well! Take time to enjoy life. Life is so short, and is full of surprises. You are not in control, so be flexible. Plan, but do not worry."

staging system) and the TNM staging system (classifying by
Tumor size, Node involvement, and extent of Metastasis). Table
4.2 shows examples of both of these systems. Both of these systems take into account several factors, such as whether the cancer is palpable (it can be felt in a DRE), the volume of
detectable cancer, local penetration into surrounding tissues,
and metastasis, or distant spreading. An accurate reading of
staging is extremely valuable for determining the method of
treatment. If the cancer is localized, that is, limited to the
prostate, then removal of the prostate could cure that person.
If the cancer has metastasized, however, other strategies must
be used to treat the cancer.

You might think that the prostate cancer starts as a small
cancer and grows bigger to encompass more and more of the
prostate. In reality, most prostate cancer starts in several spots
in the prostate. This is called multifocal disease. These multifocal spots increase in size to fill the prostate and metastasize to
other parts of the body. After biopsies are taken, the Gleason
score is determined and the number of needle cores that have
prostate cancer in them is determined. This can give an indication of the extent of spread of the cancer within the prostate.
The higher the Gleason score, the higher the likelihood that the
cancer has spread beyond the prostate. A man with extensive
cancer in multiple biopsy cores and with a Gleason score of
8–10 will have a greater likelihood of having metastatic
prostate cancer when compared to a man with less extensive
cancer of a lower Gleason score. Additionally, when the biopsy
is taken, the capsule of the prostate is part of the biopsy (see
Figure 2.3). The pathologist can look to see if the cancer
extends into or beyond the capsule. Therefore, without doing
any additional tests, the doctor can make predictions about the
degree of spread based just on the biopsy. If the man has a high
PSA (>20 ng/ml), he is also more likely to have metastatic
prostate cancer.

Metastatic prostate cancer is most common in bone (see chapter 7). If the man also complains of bone pain, that could be a sign of metastatic prostate cancer. A doctor may also do additional tests to determine if there is spread of the cancer. The most commonly used method is to do a bone scan. A bone scan is a type of x-ray that measures areas of higher metabolic activity. Since cancer cells are very metabolically active they show up as dark spots on the bone scan. There are other ways to determine the spread of the cancer, such as chest x-ray, magnetic resonance imaging, and CAT scans; however, the benefits of these over bone scans are not established.

Because we've discussed how prostate cancer is detected, graded and staged, the next chapter will discuss the main ways of treating prostate cancer.

5

Treatment of Organ-Confined Prostate Cancer

"Valley girl/ She's a valley girl/ Okay, fine/
Fer sure, fer sure/ She's a valley girl/
And there is no cure"

**From "Valley Girl" (1982) by Frank Zappa, featuring his daughter,
Moon Unit Zappa, on vocals. Frank Zappa died of prostate cancer at
age 52, December 4, 1993 (see profile, this chapter).**

There is no cure for some prostate cancer. There are very effective treatments
for prostate cancer that has not spread, or metastasized, although there is
less chance of a cure for prostate cancer when it has spread to other parts
of the body. Physicians refer to prostate cancer that has not spread as
organ-confined prostate cancer. Treatments for organ-confined prostate
cancer are often referred to as definitive local therapies. These therapies
include surgical removal of the prostate (prostatectomy), external beam
radiation, and the newer treatment brachytherapy (implantation of
radioactive seeds in the prostate, as mentioned in Darrell Bartlett's profile
at the end of the previous chapter). This chapter will further discuss
strategies for definitive local therapies.

WATCHFUL WAITING

Once a diagnosis has been made and the cancer is found to be confined to
the prostate, a decision has to be made about treatment. This decision is
often based on the extent and grade of cancer in the needle biopsy cores.
If the Gleason score is low, 2–4, and the blood PSA is below 4 ng/ml, one

choice is to elect what is called **watchful waiting**, which means to watch closely for signs of worsening disease, such as an increase in PSA or hard nodules in a DRE. Someone who chooses a watchful waiting strategy must go back to the doctor every six months. Watchful waiting can be a good choice for men who need time to decide on other treatments or who have less than 10 years' life expectancy, such as men over 75. But watchful waiting can be flirting with disaster. During the waiting period, the opportunity to completely eradicate the cancer before it has spread could be lost. Men with prostate cancer who choose surgery—or whose doctors strongly recommend it—can be treated at many major health centers by a team of physicians trained to handle particular aspects of the illness. The team can include a surgeon, a **radiation oncologist** (who specializes in radiation cancer treatments), and possibly a hematology oncologist (who specializes in pharmaceutical cancer treatments). Further information on therapeutic decision-making strategies can be found at the American Cancer Society Web site at http://www.cancer.org.

PROSTATECTOMY

Treatment of the prostate cancer surgically through the removal of the prostate may be the most straightforward strategy. If the cancer is completely confined within the prostate, then surgical removal of the prostate will definitely cure the patient of prostate cancer. The surgical technique is called **radical prostatectomy**. Figure 5.1 shows a diagram of the procedure. In a radical prostatectomy the blood supply to the prostate is stopped, the urethra is separated from the prostate where it leaves the prostate, the vas deferens is cut, and the prostate with the seminal vesicles is separated from the bladder and removed. The nerves that pass along either side of the prostate that go to the penis and control erection can sometimes be spared. The ability to spare these nerves varies considerably between different surgeons depending on

Types of Incisions

Retropubic approach

Perineal approach

Removal of Prostate: an Anatomical View

1. Dorsal vein cut and tied off to control bleeding

2. Prostate separated from urethra

3. Nerves necessary for erections spared

4. Vas deferens cut

5. Seminal vesicle removed with prostate

6. Prostate separated from bladder

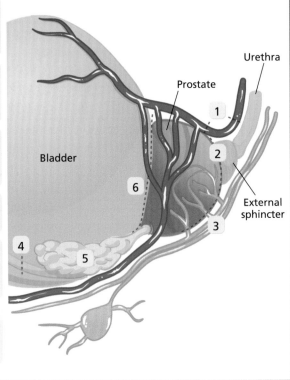

Urethra

Prostate

Bladder

External sphincter

Reconstruction of the Urinary Tract

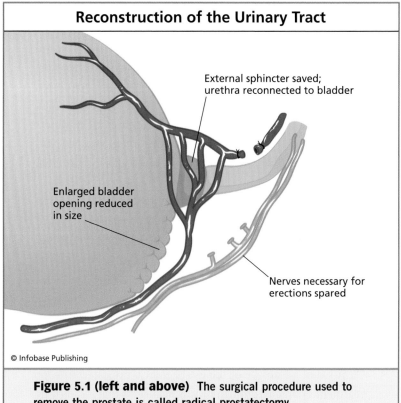

External sphincter saved; urethra reconnected to bladder

Enlarged bladder opening reduced in size

Nerves necessary for erections spared

© Infobase Publishing

Figure 5.1 (left and above) The surgical procedure used to remove the prostate is called radical prostatectomy.

their skill level, so a careful choice of surgeon is required. A typical radical prostatectomy will usually take about three hours to perform. The man is usually kept in the hospital from one to a few days. It can take six to eight weeks to fully recover from the surgery.[15] After the prostate is removed, it will be examined by a pathologist to accurately stage the disease. The pathologist pays close attention to the spread of the cancer into or through the capsule and into the seminal vesicles. This staging helps predict the likelihood that the man is cured of the cancer, and can help determine whether additional treatments should be performed (see chapter 4 for a discussion of staging).

Not everyone is a good candidate for a prostatectomy. Because this major surgery has the potential for significant blood loss, men with heart disease are generally not good candidates. In addition, men who have fewer than 10 years of life expectancy (older than 70–75, in general) may not be good candidates for surgery. A patient with metastatic prostate cancer, as indicated by a high Gleason score (8–10), is not always recommended for a radical prostatectomy. However, when there is a possibility of metastasis, many surgeons are now performing surgery on these men to treat the organ-confined cancer, and hormonal therapy follows to treat any potential metastatic prostate cancer.

Another disadvantage of prostatectomy is that if there is a preexisting but undiagnosed heart condition, there is a risk of a heart attack. My stepdad, the man profiled in chapter 8, had a preexisting blockage of several arteries in his heart. The loss of blood during surgery put extra demands on the heart, and he had a heart attack a few days after his surgery. Other disadvantages of prostatectomy are side effects of the surgery, which can include **erectile dysfunction**, **incontinence** (lack of bladder control), and bowel injury.

A major advantage of the use of radical prostatectomy for treatment of organ-confined prostate cancer is that it can com-

SUCCESS RATES OF THERAPIES

The reported success of different therapies for the treatment of organ-confined prostate cancer varies considerably depending on the study. For men with a Gleason score of 6, the five-year survival rate is about 95 percent regardless of whether they have been treated with surgery, external beam radiation, brachytherapy, or a combination. After 10 years there is a considerable amount of variation in the success rates between the different treatments, with surgery at about 90 percent. Reports of success rates for radiation can vary from 50–90 percent, and brachytherapy has not been around long enough for reliable data at 10 years.

pletely eliminate the cancer from the body. Because PSA is made exclusively by the prostate, once the prostate and the cancer are removed the PSA in the blood should go to zero. If PSA is still present after surgery, or if it begins to come back some time later, this is a helpful indication that the prostate cancer has metastasized.

EXTERNAL BEAM RADIATION

High doses of radiation are harmful to cells and can kill them, but if doses are directed carefully they can kill cancerous cells

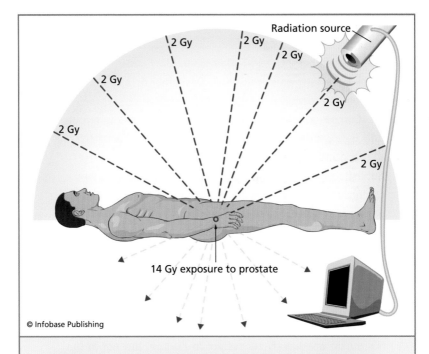

Figure 5.2 External beam radiation. A computer-operated radiation source is used to send a mathematically formulated series of focused beams directly at the prostate. Each beam by itself will not cause tissue damage, but combined the beams will kill the prostate tissue where they intersect.

in the prostate. A computer-operated machine is used to focus a beam of radiation on the prostate and to a lesser extent the adjacent tissues.[16] The beams are directed from more than one direction so that they intersect at the prostate (see Figure 5.2). By intersecting the beams the prostate gets a very high dose of radiation but the surrounding tissues get much less. The basic unit of radiation treatment is called a **gray** (**Gy**). One Gy is defined as 1 joule/kilogram of tissue. A joule is a metric unit of energy, which is equal to 4.184 calories. Each beam of radiation

FRANK ZAPPA

Born: December 21, 1940, Baltimore, Maryland
Died: Metastatic prostate cancer, December 4, 1993, Laurel Canyon, California

Composer, musician, director, satirist, and counterculture figure, Frank Zappa was an extremely creative artist who continually explored new avenues of expression. He published more 50 albums, directed several movies, and composed music in a variety of genres, including rock, pop, jazz, classical, blues, among others. He had three hit singles, "Don't Eat the Yellow Snow," "Dancing Fool," and "Valley Girl." Despite these hits, his art was never mainstream and he despised commercialism in popular music. His most well-known group, The Mothers of Invention, was an extremely influential force in 1960s underground music despite being considered a fringe act by the mainstream. His music was hugely successful in Europe, but not in the U.S. Frank Zappa, at age 53, died of advanced prostate cancer less than three years after diagnosis. More information, music samples, and photos of Frank Zappa can be found at www.zappa.com.

will typically give a dose of radiation to the prostate equal to about two Gy. Two Gy or less is usually tolerated by most tissues without significant damage. The irradiator is then moved to a new position to send another beam of two Gy irradiation. Now the prostate has received four Gy of irradiation. This process is repeated over and over until the prostate receives the desired dose, which is usually around 40–60 Gy. A computer model is used to prevent the beams from overlapping outside of the prostate.

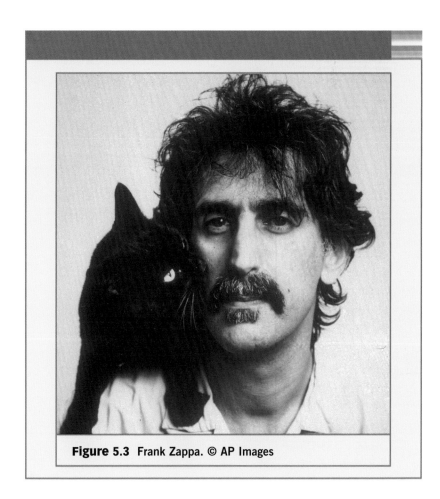

Figure 5.3 Frank Zappa. © AP Images

The treatment takes 15 to 20 minutes and is repeated five days a week for seven weeks. This regimen, or treatment program, results in killing the cells of the prostate while sparing the adjacent tissues from major injury. Note that this treatment kills both normal and cancerous prostate cells.

Radiation therapy is much less invasive than a prostatectomy. Men who are not eligible for surgery, such as those with heart disease or those with less than 10 years of life expectancy (as explained above) have radiation therapy as an option. There are also men who are eligible for surgery who choose not to have surgery for a variety of personal reasons. These men have radiation therapy as an option. Men who cannot be cured by surgery, who have metastatic prostate cancer, can be treated locally with radiation to reduce the burden of cancer. These men can also be treated at sites of metastases, areas such as those identified in bone scans.

The major advantages of radiation are that the man is able to go home between treatments and that the cure rate is similar to that of prostatectomy. A major disadvantage of radiation, however, is the lack of staging of the cancer because the prostate is not removed and analyzed by a pathologist. Generally, PSA in the blood does not go completely to zero after radiation. This residual PSA, after radiation, prevents the doctor from using PSA as a reliable test for metastatic prostate cancer.

Complications from radiation therapy include erectile dysfunction, urinary incontinence (leaking), and bowel problems. All of these problems probably result from damage to the surrounding tissue from exposure to the radiation. These problems often show up toward the end of therapy or even after therapy has been completed.

BRACHYTHERAPY

Brachytherapy is another form of radiation therapy for definitive local treatment of prostate cancer that is also known as radioactive seed implantation. Slow-release radioactive pellets are implanted into the prostate using an ultrasound-guided needle. Several pellets are implanted so that the radiation exposure of the prostate can exceed 100 to 150 Gy. The pellets remain in the prostate and are not removed. However, the radioactivity only lasts for a few months to a year, depending on the formulation. (In the profile at the end of chapter 4, Darrell Bartlett had 51 radioactive seeds implanted in his prostate.[17])

Brachytherapy can also be used in conjunction with external beam radiation to treat prostate cancer with local invasion into the surrounding tissue. The external beam radiation is administered first, and brachytherapy follows.

Brachytherapy has not been used as extensively for prostate cancer treatment as prostatectomy or external beam radiation, so the long-term cure rate is not as well documented as those therapies. However, most recent data suggest that the success of brachytherapy is as good as prostatectomy for treatment of localized prostate cancer.

A major limitation of brachytherapy is that the procedure is only available at limited locations because specialized training is required. Complications include erectile dysfunction, incontinence, and bowel problems.

A comparison of the effectiveness of different types of local definitive therapies shows that their success rates are similar. The choice of which treatment to undergo is a personal one that usually depends on several factors, which may include age, life expectancy, expertise of the doctor, and the patient's degree of comfort with a particular procedure.

6

Treatment of Advanced Prostate Cancer

"The importance of this discovery far transcends its practical implications."

Peyton Rous speaking about the pioneering work of Charles B. Huggins, which demonstrated the benefits of hormonal therapy for prostate cancer. Rous and Huggins shared the Nobel Prize in Physiology or Medicine in 1966 (Rous won for his work on tumor-inducing viruses[18]).

Hormonal therapy for prostate cancer is the most common therapeutic strategy for metastatic prostate cancer. In order to understand how this therapy works we first need to discuss the endocrine system and hormones.

HORMONES AND THE ENDOCRINE SYSTEM

Hormones are molecules made by specialized cells that control the responses of the body to the external environment and regulate normal processes of growth and differentiation. Hormones are secreted into the bloodstream where they circulate to other parts of the body to control the bodily functions. The cells that make hormones are usually located in **endocrine glands**. The prostate is an exocrine gland that secretes its contents to the outside of the body. An endocrine gland does just the opposite: It secretes its contents to the inside of the body. There are several major endocrine glands that secrete hormones to control various physiological functions. Figure 6.1 shows the major endocrine glands of the body. Table 6.1 lists the major functions of major hormones of the body.

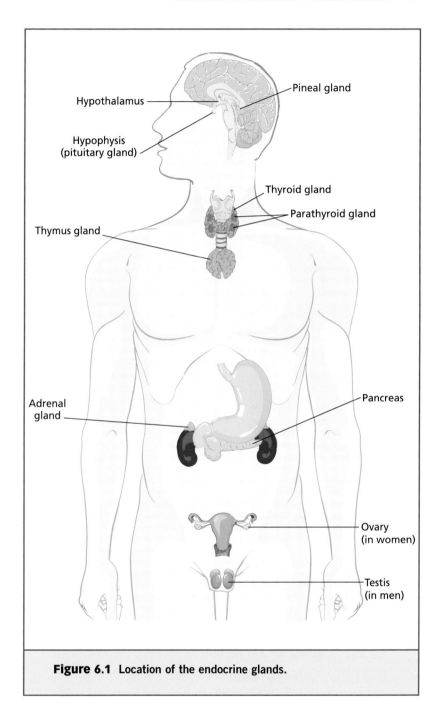

Figure 6.1 Location of the endocrine glands.

Table 6.1 Major Hormones+*

Gland	Hormone	Main Function++
Pituitary	Growth hormone	Body growth, fat metabolism
	Prolactin	Milk production, immune system
	Luteinizing hormone	Reproduction
	Follicle-stimulating hormone	Reproduction
	Thyroid-stimulating hormone	Stimulates thyroid hormone release from thyroid
	Corticotropin	Stimulates cortisol release from adrenals
Thyroid	Thyroid hormone	Growth and body temperature
	Calcitonin	Calcium homeostasis
Parathyroid	Parathryoid hormone	Calcium homeostasis
Adrenal	Cortisol	Metabolism, immune system
	Aldosterone	Sodium homeostasis
	Epinephrine	Response to danger, stress
Ovary	Estrogen	Reproduction
Testes	Androgen	Reproduction
Kidney	Vitamin D(hormone)	Calcium homeostasis, tissue differentiation
Pancreas	Insulin	Blood sugar
	Glucagon	Blood sugar

+This is a partial list of major hormones of the body.
++Most, if not all, hormones have more than one function.
*Source: Hadley, M., *Endocrinology*. Englewood Cliffs, N.J.: Prentice Hall, 1999.

Hormones regulate functions in your body such as the amount of salt or calcium in your blood, the volume of blood, reaction times (adrenaline rush), and reproductive physiology. In women this reproductive physiology involves producing an egg that is ready for fertilization (ovulation, the menstrual cycle), as well as pregnancy, mammary gland development, and lactation (milk production). In men, the same hormones promote sperm maturation, seminal vesicle functions, and prostatic functions. Reproductive hormones also control secondary sexual characteristics, including facial hair, muscle development, the location of fat accumulation, breast enlargement, among other things.

The endocrine system responds to changes in the body by regulating the amount of each hormone in the blood in a finely tuned manner. There is a balance between too much and too little of a given hormone that the body has to achieve. Regulation of hormones is often achieved by other hormones or signaling molecules produced at the target tissue where the primary hormone acts. This process is called feedback regulation. Figure 6.2 shows a simple diagram of feedback regulation.

Feedback regulation is extremely important for the concepts of **endocrinology**, and also for the use of hormonal therapy in prostate cancer. Feedback mechanisms can be quite complex. Homeostasis is the process of balancing a metabolic process, or dynamic component of the body or a cell. A simple example of feedback regulation is the regulation of blood calcium homeostasis in the body. Figure 6.3 shows an example of the processes involved in blood calcium regulation. There are three major hormones involved in the regulation of blood calcium: parathyroid hormone, calcitonin, and vitamin D_3. Although vitamin D_3 plays a major role in calcium homeostasis by increasing intestinal absorption of calcium, it has been left out of this discussion to simplify the system. Vitamin D_3 is discussed in more detail in chapter 8 because it may have a major role in prostate cancer prevention.

The body requires calcium for many processes, such as muscle contractions and enzymatic functions. Without calcium you would die, but too much calcium will result in toxic effects that can also kill you. To prevent these extremes the body has a fine-tuned system to regulate calcium. The normal range of calcium in blood plasma (the clear portion of blood after all of the cells have been removed) is between 9.5 to 11 mg

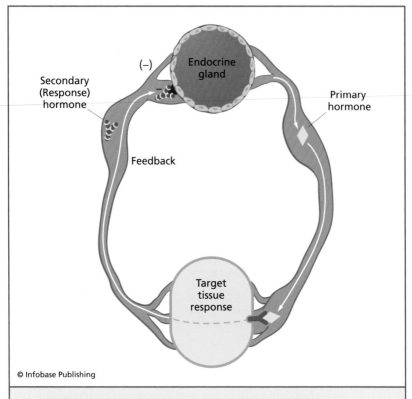

© Infobase Publishing

Figure 6.2 Feedback Regulation of Hormone Secretion.
Endocrine glands secrete hormones into the blood where they
travel to a distant tissue to elicit their actions. Most endocrine
glands receive a signal (usually another hormone) from the target
tissue that tells the endocrine gland to stop making hormones
(negative feedback).

calcium per decaliter (one tenth of a liter). Calcium is
obtained in the diet and absorbed through the gut, stored in
bone, and excreted into the urine by the kidneys. The
endocrine control of calcium homeostasis is a system that
regulates calcium absorption by the gut (vitamin D), calcium
storage or release from the bones (calcitonin and parathyroid
hormone, respectively), and calcium reabsorption from the
kidneys (parathyroid hormone).

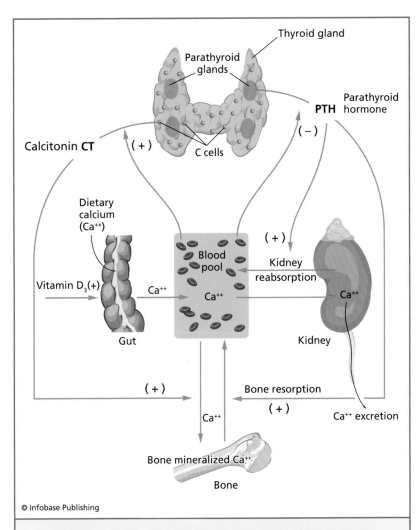

Figure 6.3 Calcium homeostasis is a simple feedback regulatory system. Calcium is absorbed by the gut after eating a meal. Increased calcium signals the C cells to turn on CT secretion (positive feedback) and the parathyroid cells to turn off PTH secretion (negative feedback). Calcitonin signals the bone cells to trap the calcium. When blood calcium levels are low then CT is shut off because of no calcium signal and the parathyroid increases PTH because the calcium is not inhibiting its secretion. PTH increases blood calcium levels at the bone and kidney.

Parathyroid hormone is made by the parathyroid glands, which are located on both sides of the thyroid gland (see Figure 6.3). Calcitonin is made in specialized cells within the thyroid gland that are called C cells. Parathyroid hormone increases blood calcium by increasing bone reabsorption of calcium and kidney reabsorption of calcium. Calcitonin decreases blood calcium by increasing calcium deposition in bone. Thus, Parathyroid hormone and calcitonin have opposite effects on blood calcium. The amount of calcium in the blood is the master regulator of parathyroid hormone and calcitonin. Figure 6.4 shows the relationships between blood calcium and blood levels of parathyroid hormone and calcitonin.

The cells of the parathyroid gland have calcium sensors (receptors) that detect the amount of calcium in the blood and send a signal to the inside of the cell. When calcium is too low, the signal is to make and secrete more parathyroid hormone. The parathyroid hormone then signals cells in the bone to release calcium from the bone and the parathyroid hormone signals the kidney to retain calcium in the body. These actions of parathyroid hormone on the bones and the kidneys result in an increase in the blood levels of calcium. As the calcium levels in the blood increase, a signal is sent to stop making and secreting parathyroid hormone.

As the calcium levels increase in the blood calcium, sensors on the C cells signal the cells to make and secrete more calcitonin. Calcitonin signals the cells of the bone to store calcium. The effects of calcitonin are to suppress the level of blood calcium. When calcium levels get below a certain threshold, the calcitonin production from the C cells is shut down and the parathyroid hormone levels from the parathyroid cells increase, starting the cycle all over again. This system results in continual adjustment of the levels of the hormones in response to the alternating increases and decreases in blood calcium.

The regulation of calcium homeostasis is relatively simple yet can respond dramatically to sudden changes in calcium. An

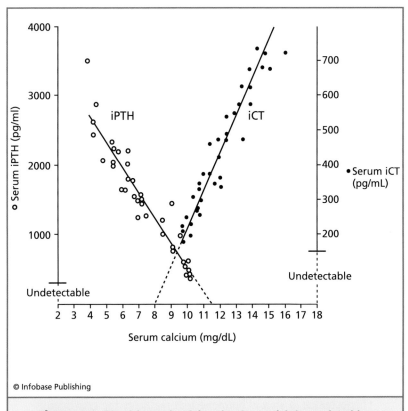

© Infobase Publishing

Figure 6.4 Blood (serum) calcium levels are tightly regulated by PTH and CT. Measurements of PTH, CT and calcium show that as calcium increases CT increases and PTH decreases.

example would be when you drink a large glass of milk. The calcium in the milk is absorbed by the gut, resulting in an increase in calcium in the blood, which promotes a release of calcitonin and a suppression of parathyroid hormone.

THE HYPOTHALAMIC-PITUITARY-TESTICULAR-PROSTATIC AXIS

Male reproductive endocrinology is a complex process. However, an understanding of this process is essential for understanding how hormonal treatment of prostate cancer works. A drawing of the hormonal control of prostate function is shown in Figure 6.3. The growth and differentiation of prostate epithelial cells is controlled by hormones. The main hormone of interest is testosterone, a steroid hormone produced by the testes called an **androgen**. All steroid hormones are derived from cholesterol. Androgens can be made by the testes and the adrenal glands located on the top of the kidneys. Another major steroid hormone is estradiol, although estra-

CHARLES BRENTON HUGGINS

Born: September 22, 1901, Halifax, Nova Scotia
Died: January 12, 1997

Charles B. Huggins won the 1966 Nobel Prize in Physiology or Medicine for his work on the use of hormonal ablation in prostate cancer. Huggins studied the physiological role of phosphorus in male fertility using the dog as a model. A series of chance discoveries combined with astute observations led to the finding that castration reduced the size of the prostate, and that adding back testosterone would make it grow again. (Testosterone, a steroid hormone that regulates the growth and development of the male reproductive system and male secondary characteristics, is produced mainly in the testes.) In his Nobel speech Huggins said, "The [normal] prostatic cell does not die in the absence of testosterone, it merely shrivels. But the hormone-dependent cancer cell is entirely different. It grows in the presence of supporting hormones but it dies in their absence." After a series of experiments involving surgical removal of testes (a procedure known as orchiectomy) in dogs with prostate cancer, Huggins began treatment of men with metastatic prostate cancer. Today hormone ablation therapy is a main tool for treating men with metastatic prostate cancer. More about Huggins, including the full text of his Nobel speech, can be found at http://nobelprize.org.

diol is not an androgen but an estrogen. Testosterone stimulates prostate luminal cell growth and enhances the production of PSA from the luminal cells. The production of testosterone from the testes is stimulated by the hormone called **lutienizing hormone** (LH) is produced by the pituitary gland, which is located at the base of the brain. Lutienizing hormone is also important in female reproductive physiology. The pituitary production of LH is in turn stimulated by gonadotropin-releasing hormone (GnRH). GnRH is sometimes called **luteinizing hormone-releasing hormone (LHRH)**. GnRH is made by a portion of the brain called the hypothalamus. The hypothalamus secretes GnRH in short bursts every 90 to 120 minutes. The GnRH binds to molecules on the surface of the pituitary cell. The molecules, called GnRH-receptors, stimulate the pituitary cell to secrete LH into the blood. The LH travels to the testes where it binds to the LH receptor, located on the surface of the testosterone-synthesizing cell called the leydig cell. The leydig cell synthesizes testosterone and secretes it locally in the testes to promote sperm production. Testosterone also travels in the blood from the testes to other sites to promote facial hair growth, muscle development, and normal prostate functions. In the prostate luminal cell, the testosterone can bind directly to its receptor, called the androgen receptor. However, the luminal cell also makes an enzyme called 5-alpha reductase. The 5-alpha reductase converts testosterone into dihydrotestosterone (DHT). DHT is much more potent than testosterone for binding to and activating the androgen receptor. **DHT is the most important hormone for the prostate.**

FEEDBACK OF TESTOSTERONE PRODUCTION

Testosterone made by the testes can travel to the hypothalamus to suppress GnRH release. It can also directly suppress LH release from the pituitary. DHT made by the prostate cells can travel to the hypothalamus and suppress GnRH release or to

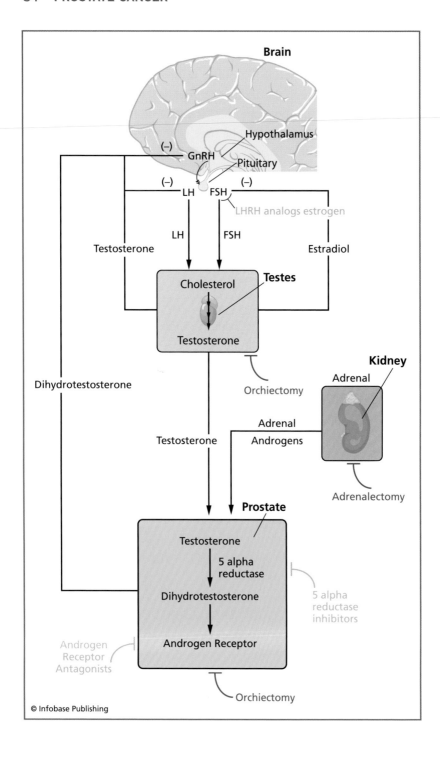

the pituitary to suppress LH release. Estradiol is also made by the testes and can travel back to the pituitary to suppress LH release. It is not clear if estradiol can suppress GnRH release from the hypothalamus. The actions of the stimulatory hormones (GnRH, LH, testosterone) are counteracted by the inhibitory effects of testicular and prostate androgens and estrogens. This system maintains a fine balance of hormones, which acts to promote optimal fertility.

HORMONE ABLATION THERAPY BY SURGERY

DHT, in addition to stimulating the normal functions of prostate luminal epithelial cells, also stimulates the growth of most prostate cancer cells. Indeed, most prostate cancer cells require androgens to stay alive. Huggins realized that if the source of testosterone was removed, then the prostate cancer might stop growing or even die. Initially this removal of testosterone was performed by simply removing the testes. Removal of the testes is called **orchiectomy, or castration**. Orchiectomy will completely remove the source of testicular androgens. Huggins showed that orchiectomy slowed the growth of the prostate cancer. However, the prostate cells have the ability to convert adrenal androgens into testosterone and then dihydrotestosterone (DHT). Huggins next removed the adrenal glands by a procedure called **adrenalectomy**. Combined orchiectomy and adrenalectomy resulted in the elimination of androgens from the body and suppression of prostate cancer

Figure 6.3 (left) The Hormonal Control of the Prostate. The prostate is dependent on androgens for normal functions. Testosterone production by the testes is controlled by a complex regulatory system that starts in the brain at the hypothalamus, next at the pituitary, then the testes. Several treatments rely on manipulation of the hypothalamic-pituitary-testicular-prostate axis. Surgical procedures are highlighted in blue and drug interventions are shown in pink. See the text for a discussion of this system.

cell growth. This pioneering work led to Huggins's winning the Nobel Prize in Physiology or Medicine in 1966.

HORMONE ABLATION THERAPY BY PHARMACEUTICAL DISRUPTORS

Modern pharmaceutical companies have developed sophisticated drugs that result in chemical castration. These drugs take advantage of the endocrine system and feedback mechanisms. Drugs have been developed that disrupt luteinizing hormone (LH) secretion from the pituitary gland, disrupt the conversion of testosterone to DHT, and block the ability of DHT to bind to the androgen receptor.

SUPPRESSION OF PITUITARY LH, LHRH, AND ESTRADIOL

Normally GnRH is secreted in a pulsating manner from the hypothalamus. This pulsing pattern of secretion is extremely important for the ability of GnRH to stimulate LH release from the pituitary. Continuous exposure of the pituitary to GnRH results in the loss of GnRH receptors on the cell surface. Without receptors, the pituitary is unable to respond to GnRH and no LH is released into the blood. Drugs called luteinizing hormone-releasing hormone analogs (LHRH analogs) have been developed that can be given in a slow-release formulation. The slow, continuous release of the drug overrides the pulsating release of the hypothalamic GnRH and prevents the release of LH from the pituitary. In the absence of LH, the leydig cells do not synthesize testosterone. In the absence of testosterone, most of the prostate cancer cells die or stop growing. Estrogen administration is also used to suppress LH release. As mentioned above, estrogen (as estradiol) is produced by the testes and feeds back to inhibit pituitary production and secretion of LH. Estrogen may also directly block prostate cell growth. Clinical injection of the synthetic estrogen diethylstilbesterol (DES) is used to suppress LH release.

ANDROGEN RECEPTOR BLOCKADE

Blocking LH production from the pituitary using LHRH or estrogen is effective at suppressing testicular testosterone production. However, it does not stop adrenal androgen production. Although adrenal androgens represent a small fraction of the total androgens in an adult male, they can have significant stimulating effects on prostate cancer cells. To effectively block both testicular and adrenal androgens, several drugs have been developed that block the ability of testosterone or dihydrotestosterone (DHT) to bind to the androgen receptor. These compounds are called antiandrogens. Most of these drugs work by mimicking the structure of DHT so that they bind to the androgen receptor instead of DHT. They have the additional ability to bind but not activate the functions of the androgen receptor. This kind of a drug is called an androgen receptor antagonist. Many androgen receptor antagonists have been developed for treatment of prostate cancer. A major advantage of these compounds over inhibitors of LH secretion is that androgen receptor antagonists block the actions of both testicular and adrenal androgens.

5-ALPHA REDUCTASE INHIBITORS

The drug class known as 5-alpha reductase inhibitors have also been developed for use to treat prostate disease. These drugs work in a similar manner to androgen receptor antagonists. They block the ability of testosterone to bind to the enzyme 5-alpha reductase. These drugs have been used extensively for the treatment of BPH to reduce the size of the prostate. They have more limited use for treatment of advanced prostate cancer because they do not completely block the actions of androgens. Although testosterone has a lesser ability to activate the androgen receptor than does DHT, it can still sometimes be potent enough to promote prostate cancer cell growth. The 5-alpha reductase inhibitor finasteride has recently been used experimentally in a large clinical trial to prevent prostate cancer.

COMBINED ANDROGEN BLOCKADE

One approach to hormonal therapy is to combine surgical castration with androgen receptor antagonists. This approach is called combined androgen blockade. The idea

HAROLD LESLIE CRAMER

Born: October 10, 1926, Boston, Massachusetts
Died: August 13, 2005, Fairfax, Virginia

When my uncle Les was diagnosed with advanced metastatic prostate cancer in spring 1988, I had just finished college and was working on breast cancer research in the Cancer Research Laboratories at the University of California–Berkeley. I was devastated. This was my first personal experience with cancer. My uncle was someone I looked up to. He was funny, intelligent, and always encouraging. I visited him that spring thinking it was probably the last time I would see him, but I had the opportunity to see Les many times after his initial diagnosis. He underwent external beam radiation therapy and hormone ablation therapy. This treatment put him in remission for 15 years—an amazing feat for someone who was considered inoperable by the surgeons. His PSA began to rise steadily a few years ago, so he chose a new experimental chemotherapy treatment with the drug docetaxol.

Les's diagnosis of prostate cancer had a major influence on my life. I had not paid particular attention to prostate cancer up to that point. It was now a disease that directly affected me. After I finished my graduate work in reproductive endocrinology, I chose to do postdoctoral research on prostate cancer.

My father was also diagnosed with prostate cancer a few years ago and underwent external beam radiation combined with brachytherapy. I now know that with my family history, I need to do everything I can to combat this disease.

is to remove all testicular androgens by castration or suppression of LH secretion and then block the actions of any remaining adrenal androgens with the androgen receptor antagonists.

Les Cramer died in his home due to complications from metastatic prostate cancer on August 13, 2005.

Figure 6.6 Harold Leslie Cramer. Courtesy the Cramer family.

DOES ANDROGEN DEPRIVATION THERAPY WORK?

Androgen deprivation effectively blocks the production and actions of androgens on prostate cancer cells, which results in reducing the growth of the cancer cells in most cases. The reduction in growth can improve the quality of life by decreasing bone pain and other complications. It may also extend the life of some men. However, this effect is usually temporary. Nearly all men undergoing androgen deprivation therapy relapse with hormone-insensitive prostate cancer. Hormone-insensitive prostate cancer can grow in the absence of androgens and is usually extremely aggressive. The two-year survival rate of men with metastatic prostate cancer undergoing androgen deprivation therapy is about 50 percent. The five-year survival rate is about 20 to 30 percent.

SIDE EFFECTS OF ANDROGEN ABLATION THERAPY

Androgen ablation therapy can have positive effects on quality of life by reducing bone pain. However, there are several undesirable side effects due to the loss of the hormone androgen. Male **libido**, the sex drive, is controlled by androgen. Nearly 100 percent of men who undergo androgen ablation therapy have decreased sex drive. **Impotence**, the inability to get an erection sufficient for intercourse, occurs in nearly 100 percent of men. For most men these are the most severe side effects. Other complications include hot flashes (about 50 percent of men), breast enlargement and/or sensitivity (about 50 percent of men), weight gain in the mid-region (about 90 percent of men). Any man contemplating androgen ablation therapy must weigh the positive and negative benefits of this treatment.

TREATMENT OF HORMONE-INSENSITIVE
PROSTATE CANCER

Unfortunately, this is still a very bleak area, with few effective treatments for hormone-insensitive prostate cancer. However, new combinations of drugs are currently being explored in clinical trials that may have benefits. One promising class of drugs is the taxol-based drugs. Taxol is a compound originally isolated from the Pacific Yew tree. This compound has potent anticancer properties. Several drug companies have made chemical modifications to taxol to reduce its side effects. Some recent clinical trials have shown that use of docetaxol, a modified taxol, can prolong the life of men with hormone-insensitive prostate cancer.

7

Spread of Prostate Cancer

Age: 60 years old.
PSA: 45 ng/ml at diagnosis in 2002; Gleason score: 10.
Tumor metastasized to bladder, kidney, and lymph nodes.
Treated with total androgen blockade.
Current PSA is 75 and rising.

This is not an unusual profile of a man diagnosed with advanced prostate cancer. As mentioned in chapter 5, if the cancer is confined to the prostate, then removal of the prostate can cure the disease. Prostate cancer localized to the prostate is rarely life-threatening. Indeed, there are many men who die with prostate cancer never diagnosed, because they lack symptoms and the cancer has not spread to other parts of the body. The metastasis of cancer is what kills men with prostate cancer. Prostate cancer can spread to most organs in the body, including the bones, lungs, liver, kidneys, and brain. Once a cancer cell has established itself at a distant site, it will gradually take over and destroy the tissue. The greatest challenge faced by doctors who treat prostate cancer is the effective treatment of metastatic prostate cancer. Research into how and why prostate cancer

Figure 7.1 (right) The steps in Metastasis. The key steps in prostate cancer metastasis are local invasion, intravasation (entry into the blood stream), survival in the blood, extravasation (exiting the blood stream), and growth at the distant tissue (in this case a vertebra).

The Steps in Metastasis

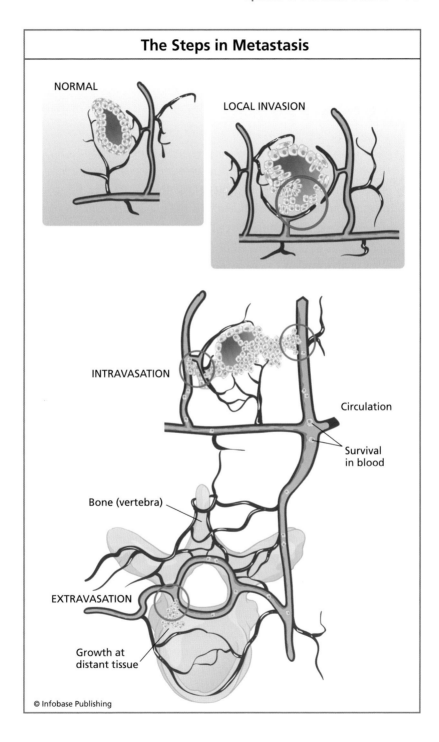

NORMAL

LOCAL INVASION

INTRAVASATION

Circulation

Survival
in blood

Bone (vertebra)

EXTRAVASATION

Growth at
distant tissue

© Infobase Publishing

spreads is leading to better methods of treatment. This chapter will explore some of the hows and whys of the metastasis of prostate cancer.

THE STEPS OF METASTASIS

Metastasis of any cancer is a complex process that requires a sequence of events to occur in the correct order. Figure 7.1 shows the main steps involved in prostate cancer metastasis. These steps are common to metastasis for any cancer, be it prostate, breast, colon, skin, etc. For the most part, each step represents a major hurdle the cell needs to overcome. If it fails, metastasis will not occur and in some cases the cell will die.[19]

Local invasion through the basal layer of cells into the surrounding stroma is the first step in metastasis. If you think about it, a normal luminal cell just sits there. It does not move. For invasion to occur, the cell has to become motile (capable of movement). Cell motility is a feature of embryonic cells and some specialized adult cells, but not normal adult prostatic epithelial cells. Some evidence suggests that motility signals from the stroma promote tumor cell migration. There also may be mutations in genes that control motility. For instance, when a cell is stuck in one place it makes proteins that literally anchor it to the surrounding cells. E-cadherin (epithelial cell adherin) sticks epithelial cells to other epithelial cells. E-cadherin expression is often lost when prostate cancer cells become invasive.

For a cell to move, it has to grab on to the surrounding cells and proteins to pull itself along. It is like having suction cups on the front of the cell that grab on, pull, and then let go. There are a number of proteins called integrins involved in the coordinated process that leads to motility. Motility is not the only thing that needs to occur for tumor cells to invade the local microenvironment. The stroma is made up of a dense, protein-rich substance primarily composed of collagen. In order for the prostate cancer cell to invade this material, it needs to secrete enzymes that actively degrade the stromal matrix. These enzymes are called proteases. Several studies have shown that invasion of prostate cells can be increased by increasing the expression of certain proteases.

Intravasation

After local invasion, the next hurdle that the cell needs to overcome is entry into the blood or lymphatic system. The process of entry into the blood system from the local microenvironment is called **intravasation**. Intravasation is almost the reverse of

WHAT IS A HYPOTHESIS?

A hypothesis is a statement that is proposed in order to explain a set of observed phenomena. In science a hypothesis is used to set a framework for future experiments. A hypothesis is usually based on the results of experiments, which can be tested by further experiments.

A theory, as used in science, is a generally accepted explanation for observed phenomena. A theory will start out as a hypothesis or perhaps a collection of hypotheses. If the hypothesis is not disproven through repeated testing, it will become generally accepted as the most plausible explanation for the phenomenon, or a theory. An example of a theory is Newton's theory of gravitation.

Hypotheses are used to drive scientific research so that defined conclusions can be drawn. For instance, Charles B. Huggins (see sidebar in chapter 6) observed that castration of a dog resulted in a regression of prostate cancer. He then hypothesized that, likewise, castration of a man would lead to regression of the man's prostate cancer. Huggins tested his hypothesis in a clinical trial (see sidebar in chapter 4) and found that his hypothesis was not proven wrong.

invasion. The basement membrane of the vessel needs to be crossed, a process that involves active protease secretion. However, the proteases that degrade the blood vessel basement membrane are not necessarily the same as the proteases involved in local invasion. The tumor cells need to grab onto and pull on the blood vessel cells (endothelial cells) using integrins.

Survival in the Circulation

Once a tumor cell arrives inside the blood it can circulate anywhere that the blood goes. However, many cells die first. Normal epithelial cells are adapted to grow attached to their neighbors. This process is called anchorage-dependent growth. If a normal cell is released from its neighbors and is allowed to float, it will die by an active process called programmed cell death, or **apoptosis** (Greek for falling off). Apoptosis is a normal way that the body programs cells to self-destruct if not in the right environment. For a cancer cell to survive in the blood, it has to escape this apoptosis by a process termed anchorage-independent growth. Anchorage-independent growth is often described as a defining feature of tumor cells. The exact signals that lead to anchorage-independent growth are not yet well understood. The tumor cell also needs to evade the immune cells in the blood. Lymphocytes, a type of white blood cell, normally capture and kill free cells in the bloodstream. The tumor cell evades capture by blocking the ability of the lymphocyte to recognize it.

Extravasation

Once survival in the bloodstream is achieved, the tumor cell has to escape from it to establish growth at a distant site. The process of leaving the blood vessels and entering a tissue is called **extravasation**. This process is very much the reverse of intravasation. What stops a cell from circulating is a matter of considerable debate. There is some evidence that the endothelial cells that line the blood vessels express different integrins, depending on the tissue that the blood vessel is in. The cancer cells have a preference for certain integrins over others. The cancer cell binds to the endothelial cells expressing its preferred integrins and stops circulating. It then can undergo the process of extravasation.

METASTATIC GROWTH

The tumor cell does not automatically begin to grow at a metastatic site. The local tissue has to be invaded through active proteolytic degradation of the matrix, the cell has to re-adapt to a more sedentary existence, and the cell may also have to overcome signals from the local tissue that actively inhibit tumor cell growth. Sometimes a cancer cell may metastasize to a distant site but just sit there for years, lying dormant until signals change or it acquires mutations that allow it to grow again.

PROSTATE CANCER METASTASIS

Metastasis to bone occurs in 95 percent of men who have metastatic prostate cancer, making bone the most common site. Lung metastases rank second, being found in about 50 percent of men. Liver ranks third, with 25 percent. Brain metastases are rare and other sites are extremely rare. What makes prostate cancer have different preferences for metastatic sites? No one really knows. However, some good hypotheses have been proposed. One possibility, mentioned above, is that the endothelial cells that line the blood vessels express integrins that allow for attachment of the prostate cells. This hypothesis would argue that bone endothelial cells express the stickiest surface for prostate cells of any tissue. Indeed, there is considerable evidence to support the hypothesis that prostate cells preferentially stick to bone. Bone happens to be a very rich source of growth factors. Growth factors are like hormones except that they work in the same tissue in which they are made. When the bone-building cells called osteoblasts make new bone, they also make growth factors that get stuck in the hardened, or mineralized, bone. When the bone is broken down by the bone-destroying cells called osteoclasts, these embedded growth factors are released and can stimulate local cell growth. The prostate may take advantage of this growth factor–rich environment and use it to help it establish a bone metastasis.

TREATMENT OF METASTATIC PROSTATE CANCER

Metastatic prostate cancer is a difficult disease to treat. Organ-confined prostate cancer can be treated by local therapy such as surgery or external beam radiation. With metastatic prostate cancer, surgery is usually not an option because the disease can be embedded in tissues that cannot be removed, such as bone, lung, or liver. Radiation has some limited uses when the location of the metastatic site is known. However, it is often impossible to identify the location(s) of the cancer. The main tool to treat metastatic prostate cancer is hormone ablation therapy. This therapy and its associated benefits and side effects are discussed in detail in chapter 6. There is also a limited role for chemotherapy, also discussed in chapter 6.

PREDICTING AND DETECTING THE SPREAD OF PROSTATE CANCER

At the time of diagnosis a considerable amount of effort goes into predicting whether the prostate cancer has spread beyond the prostate. This information is used to help the doctor and patient decide on the treatment strategy. A bone scan can directly visualize the presence of metastatic prostate cancer. However, this technique can miss a lot of cancers. Bone scans can detect relatively large mestastases, but are unable to detect small metastases. (As discussed in chapter 3, the primary tool to predict metastases is the needle core biopsies, using Gleason scoring. The higher the Gleason score, the more aggressive the cancer is and the more likely it will have spread beyond the prostate.) Another, more direct determination is whether the capsule that surrounds the prostate has been penetrated by the cancer. Another predictor is the blood level of PSA at diagnosis. If the level of PSA is above 10 ng/ml (see chapter 3), then there is a high likelihood of metastatic cancer. The higher the blood level of PSA, the more likely there is metastatic prostate cancer.

If the prostate has been removed by surgery, the pathologist can determine the amount of cancer, the Gleason score, and if there is invasion into the seminal vesicles. All of these measures help the pathologist stage the cancer and predict if metastasis has occurred (see chapter 3 for more discussion). After a prostatectomy, the blood level of PSA should rapidly drop to zero if there are no metastatic prostate cancer cells. If PSA blood levels remain elevated after prostatectomy, then this is an indication of prostate cancer metastasis.

BIOCHEMICAL RELAPSE

The recurrence of prostate cancer after definitive local therapy such as prostatectomy or radiation therapy is known as **relapse**. As mentioned before, after prostatectomy or radiation treatment the PSA level will drop to near zero. However, this does not mean that there are no hidden metastases. Hidden metastases may be so small that they do not contribute to blood levels of PSA. After local therapy, the man goes back to his doctor every six months and then every year for a checkup. This checkup will include measurement of blood PSA levels. If there is a metastasis that grows large enough to contribute to blood levels of prostate specific antigen, the PSA test will detect this. An increasing PSA level in the blood without any other symptoms is called **biochemical relapse**. However, often there is some natural variation in the base level of PSA that complicates interpretation of the PSA test. You will remember that even though the prostate is the major source of PSA, other tissues can make minute amounts. Because of these natural variations in the base level of prostate specific antigen, more than one PSA measurement separated by at least a month is required to make a diagnosis of relapse. Most doctors want at least three consecutive PSA increases before they will give a diagnosis of biochemical relapse.

WATCH OUT FOR SIGNS OF PROSTATE CANCER AND ACT ON THEM

NORTON ERNEST
Born: 1921, in a tiny Minnesota village on the shores of the Mississippi

Norton spent his early teenage years as a Tom Sawyer–like "river rat." At 17 he took a Minnesota–Canadian wilderness canoe trip with a close friend. This trip made a lasting impression on Norton. After graduating from the University of Minnesota he enlisted in the Army in 1942, where he served three and a half years. After a short business career in Minneapolis, he moved to California in 1952. He was CEO for several northern California hospitals and retired from National Medical Enterprises as a vice president for Hospital Development in 1982.

Norton's prostate cancer was detected after he noticed blood in his urine and his frequent urination at night. A PSA blood test was high (37). Needle biopsy of the prostate confirmed the presence of cancer, with a Gleason score 7. Norton underwent two separate surgical procedures and completely changed his lifestyle, eliminating high-fat meats and other risky foods, substituting soy products, fish, and turkey. After 15 years he remains free of detectable prostate cancer.

He currently is an activist for promoting awareness of prostate cancer. He was the first chairman for the Prostate Cancer Initiative for the American Cancer Society's northern California, Mountain Valley region. For 10 years he has been the facilitator of a large Man to Man support group. He also presents to newly diagnosed men on the basics of prostate

In the absence of any other symptoms, such as bone pain, what, if anything, should be done if biochemical relapse is detected? There is considerable controversy over what should be done. If the PSA is still low, less than 2 or 3 ng/ml, many

cancer. In 2005 Norton was one of two Californians awarded the prestigious St. George National Award by the American Cancer Society for his 12 years of service to cancer patients. It is the highest recognition that can be given a volunteer and must have the endorsement of both the state and national boards of the American Cancer Society.

Figure 7.2 Norton Ernest. Courtesy Norton Ernest.

people opt to do nothing. The rate of increase in PSA is also a factor. If the PSA takes two years to double (called the doubling time), there is less cause for concern than if the doubling time is three months. Treatment options are the same as those discussed in chapter 6.

Metastatic prostate cancer represents the end stage of a disease progression that begins with PIN (see chapter 3) and progresses through locally invasive disease. Once metastases have occurred, it is a struggle to rid the body of cancer. The ideal situation is to prevent the cancer from spreading in the first place. The next chapter will discuss the role of prevention in prostate cancer.

8

Prostate Cancer Prevention

While advanced metastatic prostate cancer has no cure at this time, prevention of this deadly disease is the best way to "cure" it now. There are two questions to ask: What are the ways to prevent prostate cancer, and when should preventive actions start?

Now is the time to prevent the factors leading to the disease, no matter what age you are. Men should start thinking about, and acting on, ways to prevent prostate cancer. Women can encourage all the men they know to start now. Men can make these changes at any age. Whether 16 or 46 years old, now is the best time to start a prevention strategy. Prevention is really about subtle lifestyle changes. It is never too early or too late to start a prevention program.

Most cancer probably occurs from the amount of exposure of the person to chemicals or substances in the environment that either cause cancer—and, conversely, cancer might fail to occur from the amount of exposure a man has to carcinogens (substances that cause cancer). The substances that prevent cancer we will call prevention agents. The balance between the amounts of exposure to carcinogens and to prevention agents will determine a person's risk of getting cancer. More carcinogens and less prevention agents equals a higher risk. If you know what these carcinogens and prevention agents are, then you could change your risk.

The study of patterns of human disease in different populations is called **epidemiology**. Populations can be divided into what country they live in, how long they lived in a certain neighborhood, the food they eat, how much sun they get, the job they have, how close to the equator they live, how many sexual partners they have had, and other factors. All of this information can be sorted by whether the person gets a certain disease or not. Statistical equations are used to calculate the association of a certain disease with a certain population pattern. For instance, people who are obese have a higher incidence of heart disease. At any given age, men have a higher incidence of heart disease than do women. Obese men have a much higher risk for cardiovascular disease than average-sized women.

Another association that has been demonstrated by epidemiology is the association of lung cancer with people who smoke cigarettes. To demonstrate these associations with a high degree of scientific certainty, an epidemiologist will collect information from thousands, even tens of thousands, of people selected randomly. Statistical tests are then performed on the data. The quality and accuracy of the predictions from the epidemiological study are dependent on the quality and accuracy of the population data collected.

Anecdotal stories are another way that people look at causes of disease. An example would be the following made-up scenario: Joe has prostate cancer. Joe was an avid bicycle rider. He rode his bicycle across the United States when he was in college, and raced mountain bikes. He rides his bicycle to work every day and he goes on 50- to 100-mile rides on weekends. All that pressure on the prostate from sitting on the hard bicycle seat probably gave him prostate cancer. In fact, Joe learned last week that two men in his cycling club also got prostate cancer. It appears that bicycle riding must cause prostate cancer.

The association of bicycle riding with prostate cancer as described above is anecdotal. How is this different from epidemiology? Epidemiologists collect very detailed information about people in a population—information on all aspects of lifestyle such as diet, income, age, weight, ethnicity, other diseases, and family history, among other factors.. They also are interested as much in the people who do not get the disease as in the people who do get the disease. For instance, in the scenario above, epidemiologists would want to study the men in the cycling group who did not get prostate cancer. Also, if epidemiologists were to look at a non-bicycle riding population of men of comparable age, weight, socioeconomic status, ethnicity, and family history, they would want to determine if there would be more or fewer cases of prostate cancer in this control group (meaning a group of similar populations—the non-bike riders) except for the factors undergoing study). An epidemiological study tries to control for all of these factors and more to make predictions about the causes of disease. It should be emphasized that by either an anecdotal or an epidemiological method, an association between lifestyle and presence of disease is made.

It has been established that age, race, and family history are the major risk factors for getting prostate cancer. These three risk factors were identified by epidemiology. However, you cannot change these factors: They are fixed and are not modifiable by prevention strategies. In addition to these fixed risk factors, solid associations for causal or preventive agents for prostate cancer are limited. A number of lifestyle exposures have been proposed as causative agents based mostly on anecdotal or poorly designed epidemiological studies. High-quality epidemiological studies have demonstrated no association of these factors with the development of prostate cancer. Some factors that have been proposed but are unlikely to have a role in prostate cancer are cigarettes, coffee, promiscuous sexual activity, alcohol, bicycle riding, and vasectomy. Some potential carcinogens, such as cadmium and chlorinated pesticides, can be associated with prostate cancer. Yet little is known about which carcinogens are major factors in prostate cancer. In terms of prevention, avoiding exposure to these chemicals is the first strategy. It certainly cannot hurt to avoid them. Dietary factors are the easiest to change and the most is known about them.

SOY POWER

Asian men, particularly men from China and Japan, have some of the lowest rates of prostate cancer of any population. As mentioned in chapter 1, the incidence rate in prostate cancer rose for Japanese men who have immigrated to Hawaii and then to the United States. Epidemiologists have been studying differences in lifestyles between men in the United States and Japanese and Chinese men for several decades. One major factor has been identified as an important role in preventing prostate cancer: soybean products, such as tofu and soy milk. The Japanese diet is very rich in soy products while the typical Western diet is relatively low in soy products. There are many good epidemiological studies that associate soy with decreased prostate cancer risk. Researchers have investigated the possible causal link between dietary soy consumption and low prostate cancer risk. Most research has focused on a particular compound, called an isoflavone because of its chemical structure, found in high quantities in soybeans. Interestingly, many isoflavones have chemical structures similar to estrogens and are often called phytoestrogens (*phyto* meaning plant). A comparison of the chemical structures of estradiol and a common soy isoflavone called genistein is shown in Figure 8.1.

Laboratory research has shown that genistein can bind to the estrogen receptor. As discussed in chapter 6, estrogen inhibits pituitary release of LH and is sometimes used in prostate cancer therapy. Estrogen may also have more direct effects of inhibiting prostate cell growth. One could guess that genistein may do the same thing. Indeed, genistein will inhibit prostate cell growth in experimental systems. In experimental animal models genistein can inhibit prostate cancer development. What is not clear is whether genistein inhibits prostate cancer in humans. Preliminary studies in people have been inconclusive. To test this, a large clinical trial would have to be conducted where thousands of young men are fed soy for years and then the incidence of prostate cancer is determined at the

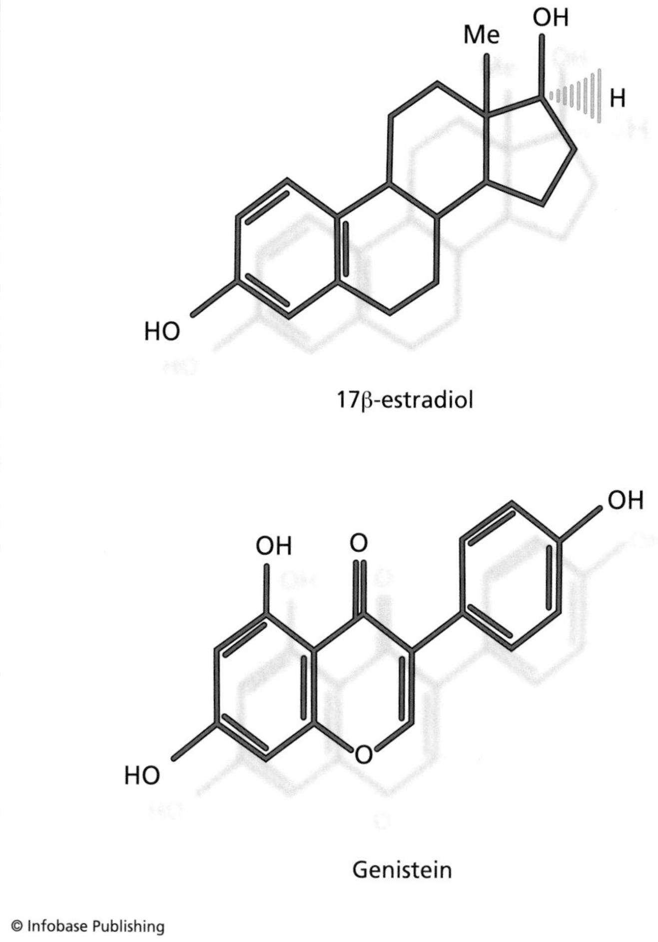

OH
Me
H

HO

17β-estradiol

OH

OH   O

HO

O

Genistein

© Infobase Publishing

Figure 8.1 Comparative Structures of Genistein and Estradiol. These chemical structures show how similar estradiol and genistein are. Genistein possesses many characteristics of an estrogen.

end of the study. Remember, prostate cancer is mostly a disease of older men. However, the beginnings may happen at a very young age. No one has yet proposed to conduct a clinical trial that lasts 50 years. We may never know by a well-conducted study whether soy supplementation can prevent the development of prostate cancer in men. However, it is easy enough to include soy in your diet, and if it could reduce your risk of getting prostate cancer, then why not consider soy-based products as part of your diet?

VITAMIN D AND SUN

Perhaps the best epidemiological data for risk factors and prostate cancer is the exposure to sun. Epidemiological studies have shown a direct correlation of sun exposure and skin cancer. Ultraviolet (UV) rays from the sun penetrate the outer layers of skin to turn the deep layer of skin cells into skin cancer cells. Dermatologists have been warning about the correlation between sun and skin cancer for decades—particularly if you have fair skin. Now we cover up when we go out in the sun, slap on sunblock, and we lower our risk for developing deadly skin cancer.

However, for prostate cancer the opposite is true: The less the sun exposure, the higher the risk of developing prostate cancer. The first hint of this inverse correlation came from work by Gary Schwartz while he was a graduate student at the University of North Carolina at Chapel Hill. Dr. Schwartz was looking at prostate cancer incidence, county by county, in every single county in the United States. He also had very good environmental data on the amount of sun exposure on a county-by-county basis. What he found is shown in Figure 8.2. There is a linear trend in the incidence of prostate cancer in a south-to-north direction. Men in the South have a lower incidence of prostate cancer than do men in the North (Figure 8.3). When he plotted the amount of sun exposure (UV index), he came up with the reverse trend. The data plotted together showed an inverse correlation between sun exposure and prostate cancer risk.

You may be wondering how the sun could affect cancer in an internal organ like the prostate. Dr. Schwartz recognized

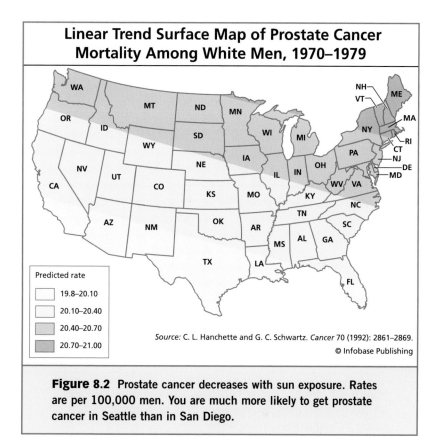

Linear Trend Surface Map of Prostate Cancer Mortality Among White Men, 1970–1979

Predicted rate

19.8–20.10

20.10–20.40

20.40–20.70

20.70–21.00

Source: C. L. Hanchette and G. C. Schwartz. *Cancer* 70 (1992): 2861–2869.

© Infobase Publishing

Figure 8.2 Prostate cancer decreases with sun exposure. Rates are per 100,000 men. You are much more likely to get prostate cancer in Seattle than in San Diego.

that the pattern of prostate cancer in the United States mimicked the pattern of a disease that was very prevalent in Europe during the industrial revolution. This ailment, called rickets, is a disease of vitamin D deficiency. Vitamin D, which is actually a hormone, requires skin exposure to the sun as a critical step in its synthesis. Rickets was common in the industrial revolution of the 1800s because of a lack of sun exposure from long hours workers spent in coal-burning factories and the extreme air pollution expelled from those factories. In the section on calcium homeostasis in chapter 6, vitamin D was mentioned as being important for calcium absorption. Without vitamin D, bones are not formed properly due to calcium insufficiency.

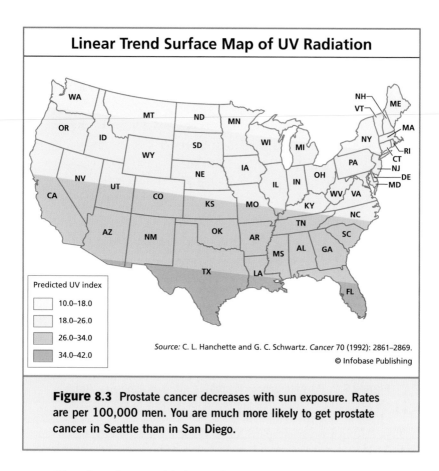

Linear Trend Surface Map of UV Radiation

Predicted UV index

- 10.0–18.0
- 18.0–26.0
- 26.0–34.0
- 34.0–42.0

Source: C. L. Hanchette and G. C. Schwartz. *Cancer* 70 (1992): 2861–2869.

© Infobase Publishing

Figure 8.3 Prostate cancer decreases with sun exposure. Rates are per 100,000 men. You are much more likely to get prostate cancer in Seattle than in San Diego.

Vitamin D is now added to milk and other foods as a preventive to the development of rickets.

Figure 8.4 shows a diagram of the vitamin D endocrine system in relation to the prostate. Cholesterol in the skin is converted to vitamin D_3 by the exposure of the skin to UV from the sun. Vitamin D_3 is not the active hormone. It must first travel to the liver, where it is converted to prohormone D, and then to the kidneys where it is modified to the active vitamin D_3 hormone, which I will call Hormone D to distinguish it from vitamin D_3 that is the precursor made in the skin. Without sunlight, your body relies on dietary vitamin D_3. Milk has small amounts of vitamin D_3 added to it. Fish, particularly deep-sea fish like tuna and skipjack, have very high levels of vitamin D_3. For instance, the amount of vitamin D_3 added to a quart of milk is 400 international units (IU). One gram (less than a teaspoon) of skipjack oil can have as much as 80,000 IUs of vitamin D_3.

For many decades, the only recognized role for Hormone D was in calcium regulation and proper bone formation.[20] However, research conducted over the last 20 to 30 years has shown that Hormone D has a number of other effects on cells in the body, particularly as an important regulator of epithelial cell growth and differentiation. We now know from several studies conducted in cell culture and in animal models that Hormone D inhibits prostate cell growth and at the same time stimulates more differentiated cells in the prostate. There are now numerous well-conducted epidemiological studies that have verified the original studies of Gary Schwartz that show an inverse correlation between sunlight and prostate cancer risk. Some studies have gone further to measure actual prohormone D and Hormone D levels in the blood of men. Men who have prostate cancer are more likely to have lower levels of prohormone D and Hormone D in the blood.

There are no clinical studies that have used any sort of vitamin D for prostate cancer prevention. However, some small clinical trials have been conducted using Hormone D to treat existing prostate cancer. The results are promising. Michael Hollick, a professor at Boston University, suggests that a few minutes a day in the sun is long enough to synthesize enough vitamin D_3 to prevent prostate cancer as well as a number of other diseases.[21] This assumes that you are not wearing sunscreen and it also depends on your skin color, the time of year, and distance from the equator. This suggestion makes dermatologists uneasy because of the perceived risk for increase in skin cancer. However, there is a large body of scientific data that supports a role for vitamin D in the prevention of several cancer types besides prostate cancer, particularly breast and

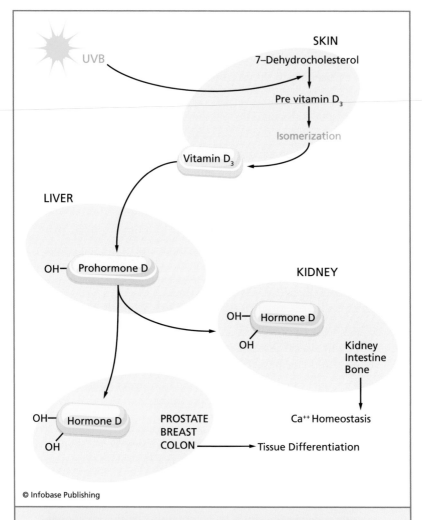

Figure 8.4 Vitamin D Synthesis. Vitamin D synthesis by your body requires sun exposure to skin to start the process. Vitamin D₃ is then converted to Prohormone D (25 hydroxyvitamin D₃). Prohormone D goes to the kidney to be made into Horomone D (1,25-dihydroxyvitamin D3). Hormone D produced by the kidney regulates calcium homeostasis. Prohormone D can also be turned into Hormone D by the prostate, where it inhibits cell growth and promotes tissue differentiation. Hormone D can also be made by the breast and colon.

colon cancer. Everything in moderation: The risk is still there, however, and I recommend caution before soaking up the rays with unprotected skin. Yet if everyone were to go out in the sun for 15 minutes, it could be possible that the potential number of lives saved by preventing breast, colon and prostate cancer could far exceed the small number of lives lost to skin cancer.

Dietary supplementation of vitamin D_3 (not prohormone D or Hormone D) is perhaps an ideal means of preventing prostate cancer. It can easily be added to the diet through tasty natural sources such as salmon or tuna. It is inexpensive to supplement with vitamin D capsules, which can be purchased from pharmacies or health food stores for pennies a day. Finally, vitamin D_3 is safe (although too much can be toxic, as discussed below). Your body has a very tightly controlled feedback regulation system (see chapter 6), to modulate the amount of blood Hormone D it makes. Putting more vitamin D_3 into your body does not equal more Hormone D in the blood. Once the blood levels of Hormone D reach a certain set point, the synthesis of Hormone D is shut off, even if there is excess vitamin D_3. What is so amazing about vitamin D_3 and prostate is that prostate cells can make their own Hormone D! Prostate cells take prohormone D (made by the liver from vitamin D_3) and convert it to Hormone D, just as the kidneys do. But the synthesis of Hormone D in the prostate does not contribute to blood levels of Hormone D and is not regulated like the synthesis of Hormone D from the kidneys. Therefore, you can safely take much larger doses of vitamin D_3 than you can Hormone D. Unlike the kidneys where there is a set point for the amount of Hormone D made, the prostate cells do not seem to have this same set point. The more vitamin D_3 you take in from the diet or from sun exposure, the more the prohormone D is made in the liver, and then the more the Hormone D is made in the prostate. Research has shown that Hormone D manufactured by the prostate will inhibit unhealthy prostate cell growth.

How much is enough? Although vitamin D_3 is fairly safe, it can be toxic if taken in large quantities, so do not overdo it. The recommended daily allowance of vitamin D_3 is 200 international units (IU) for children and adults up to 49 years old, 400 IU for adults 50 to 70 years old, and 600 IU older than 70.

SELENIUM AND VITAMIN E CANCER PREVENTION TRIAL (SELECT)

With a participant population of 35,534 men, SELECT (Selenium and Vitamin E Cancer Prevention Trial) is the largest-ever prostate cancer prevention trial.[22] Participants are 55 and older, and 50 and older for African-American men.

The main objective of the study is to determine whether selenium or vitamin E, alone or in combination, will prevent the incidence of clinical prostate cancer. Several secondary objectives are also included, such as the effects on lung and colon cancers, cardiovascular disease, Alzheimer's disease, and macular degeneration.

Men are randomly assigned to four groups. Group 1 will take two placebo pills a day; group 2 will take one selenium and one placebo pill a day; group 3 will take one vitamin E and one placebo pill a day; group 4 will take one selenium and one vitamin E pill a day. Men will be on this trial for seven to 12 years.

This is a double-blind trial, that is, the men in the study do not know what pills they are taking and the doctors running the study do not know what pills the men are taking. This is done to prevent bias in the study. Each patient is coded. At the end of the study the code is cracked and the doctors then know who got the drug and who got the placebo.

This study is sponsored by the National Cancer Institute and run by the Southwest Oncology Group. More information about this and other clinical trials for cancer can be found at http://www.cancer.gov/clinicaltrials.

This minimal amount of vitamin D_3 is the amount known to prevent rickets. The levels required to prevent rickets may be significantly lower than the amount required to prevent prostate and other cancers. Michael Hollick recommends in *The UV Advantage*[23], 1000 IU per day. According to the National Academy of Sciences, the upper recommended safe dose of vitamin D_3 is 2000 IU per day.[24] Beyond these levels there is danger of vitamin D_3 toxicity.

HIGH FAT/LOW FAT—GOOD FAT/BAD FAT

The increase in obesity in the United States has gained a lot of attention. Obesity has been linked to a number of diseases

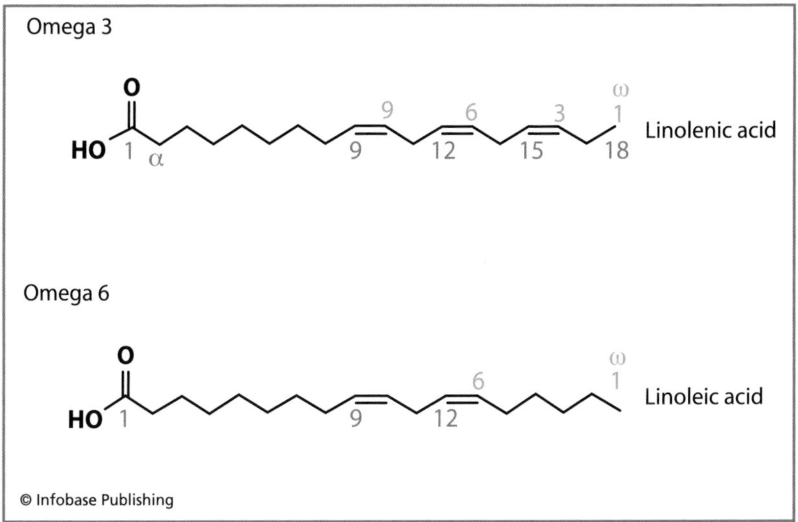

© Infobase Publishing

Figure 8.5 Chemical structure of alpha-linolenic acid, an essential omega-3 fatty acid, and alpha linoleic acid, a comparable omega-6 fatty acid. Although chemists count from the carbonyl carbon (blue numbering), physiologists count from the omega ω carbon (red numbering). Note that for linolenic acid, from the omega end (diagram right), the first double bond appears as the third carbon-carbon bond (line segment), hence the name "omega-3."

including heart disease, diabetes, and several types of cancer. There is still considerable controversy about the role of a high-fat diet in the risk for prostate cancer. Some studies have shown a correlation, while others have not. More recently, attention has been focused on the particular type of fat and the ratios of these different types of fats. Fats from different sources have different chemical and biological properties. At first the focus was on saturated versus unsaturated fats. Animal meats, particularly red meats, are high in saturated fats, while vegetable fats tend to be high in unsaturated fats. However, vegetables contain some saturated fats and red meats contain some unsaturated fats. The association of fat with prostate cancer based on these general assumptions has been weak at best.[25]

MEN WITH PROSTATE CANCER DIE OF OTHER CAUSES

STANLEY JOY ODMANN
Born: San Francisco, California, December 28, 1932.
Died: May 11, 2005, from complications from pancreatic cancer after surviving prostate and throat cancer as well as quadruple bypass surgery.

Stan's prostate cancer was detected by routine PSA screening, followed by positive biopsy. He underwent successful surgery and remained PSA-negative for 10 years before his death. Stan's history of prostate cancer is typical for many men who are diagnosed early. He did not die from prostate cancer but from other causes.

Stan had a distinguished career as a San Francisco police officer. He retired as sergeant of the Solo Motorcycles department in 1987. Stan was accomplished at the restoration of antique motorcycles, airplanes, cars, and trucks to pristine condition. His last project was a 1950 Studebaker truck. Even after his diagnosis with pancreatic cancer, he worked passionately to complete the restoration of the Studebaker.

A lot of recent attention has been focused on the amounts of two types of unsaturated fats called omega-3 and omega-6 fats. The difference between omega-3 and omega-6 fats are in the location of a kind of chemical bond called a double bond. Omega-3 fats have the bond in the number 3 position and omega-6 fats have the bond in the number 6 position. Figure 8.5 shows the chemical structures of common omega-3 and omega-6 fats. Your body cannot make fats with the bond in the number 3 position but needs to get these fats from the diet. Omega-3 fats are found in high quantities in fish such as salmon and tuna, as well as canola oil and flax seeds. Red meat, on the other hand, is very low in omega-3 and high in omega-6 fats. Some omega-6 fats are made into hormones or growth

Figure 8.6 Stanley Odmann. Courtesy the author.

factors that can stimulate cell growth. Some omega-3 fats are made into molecules that inhibit cell growth. There are now a few well-conducted epidemiological studies that show an association of high omega-3 fats with decreased prostate cancer risk. Most of the evidence suggests that the main effect occurs when the ratio of omega-3 to omega-6 is shifted in favor of omega-3 fats. These epidemiological results are very promising and suggest that eating fish (in substitution for red meat) two to three times a week could alter the ratio of omega-3 to omega-6 fats and contribute to the prevention of prostate cancer. Further experimental work using laboratory models is needed to support a large-scale clinical trial to test the prevention of prostate cancer by omega-3 fats. In the meantime it cannot hurt to eat more fish, cook with canola oil, and sprinkle some flax seeds on your cereal.

A LITTLE KETCHUP ON YOUR GRAPEFRUIT?

One particularly strong and unexpected finding from several well-conducted epidemiological studies is the finding that consumption of tomato products reduces the risk of prostate cancer. Cooked tomatoes are better than raw tomatoes. Pasta with red sauce, pizza, tomato soup, lasagna—anything with cooked tomatoes, even ketchup, is associated with a decrease in prostate cancer risk. These epidemiological studies look at detailed eating habits of men. Further study has identified a specific compound called lycopene that is found in high concentrations in tomatoes. Lycopene is a red pigment with antioxidant properties. It is also found in other fruits, such as watermelons, papaya, guava, and pink grapefruit. Two servings of cooked tomatoes a week may reduce the risk of developing prostate cancer by nearly 30 percent. Animal studies have supported the epidemiological findings.

SELENIUM AND VITAMIN E

Selenium is a mineral found in drinking water, meats, seafood, and plants (for example, brazil nuts). A clinical trial that was designed to look at the effects of selenium on skin cancer showed a 50 percent reduction in prostate cancer. Interestingly, no effect of selenium on skin cancer incidence was observed. Selenium can act as a strong antioxidant and may be concentrated in the prostate. Vitamin E is another antioxidant that is found in a number of foods, including vegetables, vegetable oil, and egg yolk. A large clinical trail that was designed to look at the effects of vitamin E on lung cancer incidence in smokers showed a 32 percent reduction in prostate cancer. Other epidemiological studies have supported a role of vitamin E in reducing prostate cancer risk. Based on these findings the National Cancer Institute has initiated the largest clinical trial designed to look at prevention of a cancer. The SELECT trial will test the preventive effects of selenium and vitamin E will be tested in more than 35,000 men for seven to 12 years (see the sidebar in this chapter). The results of this trial could direct the future of prostate cancer prevention research.

OTHER FACTORS

There are a number of other factors that have been considered in cancer prevention in general that should be considered here. The consumption of fresh fruits and vegetables, although not directly associated with prostate cancer, may contribute a general benefit for cancer prevention. Cruciferous vegetables in particular may be of great benefit. Cruciferous vegetables include broccoli, cauliflower, brussels sprouts, kale, among others. Calcium, although good for your bones, may be bad for your prostate. Some very good epidemiology suggests that high calcium intake is associated with increased prostate cancer. Grilling meats on the barbecue is known to produce carcinogens and has been linked to colon cancer. Although there is no direct link to prostate cancer with people who eat a lot of grilled meats, it may be wise to reduce the amount of grilled meats eaten.

PREVENTION STRATEGIES

There is no single, sure-fire measure that is known to prevent prostate cancer. However, there are several things that could be changed in the average American lifestyle that may significantly reduce the risk of prostate cancer development. The changes below are my recommendations. These changes should not be done all at once. Rather, a gradual shift in the focus of the diet will result in more lasting changes.

1. Eat a well-balanced diet rich in fruits and vegetables. Strive for at least five servings of fruits and vegetables a day. Look for alternatives rich in lycopene, such as tomato-based sauces, grapefruit, and watermelon. Increase the amount of cruciferous vegetables.

2. Reduce intake of fat and particularly fat from red meat. Substitute two to three servings of fish a week for red meat. Cook with canola or olive oil.

3. Add soy-based foods to your diet.

4. Supplement your diet with at least 1000 IU of vitamin D_3 per day, but do not exceed 2000 IU per day.

5. Avoid or minimize exposure to carcinogens (cadmium and pesticides) and reduce the amount of grilled meat.

How can these changes be made in today's fast-paced world? It comes down to thinking about what to eat and making choices. Bring a banana or an apple as a dessert for lunch instead of a bag of chips. When eating out, choose the fish rather than the beef. Explore new options such as soy milk. Make changes a little at a time. These changes will certainly not hurt you and may save your life.

1. American Cancer Society. "Cancer Facts and Figures 2006." Available online. URL: http://www.cancer.org/. Accessed June 5, 2006.
2. American Cancer Society. "Cancer Facts and Figures 2006." Available online. URL: http://www.cancer.org/. Accessed June 5, 2006.
3. See the National Cancer Institute Web site for more about genes. National Cancer Institute. "Gene Testing." Available online. URL: http://www.cancer.gov/cancertopics/UnderstandingCancer/genetesting. Accessed June 5, 2006.
4. More information can be found in chapter 8 and on the National Cancer Institute Web site. National Cancer Institute. "Prostate Cancer: Prevention, Genetics, Causes" Available online. URL: http://www.cancer.gov/cancertopics/ prevention-genetics-causes/prostate. Accessed June 5, 2006.
5. Cunha, G., A. Donjacour, P. Cooke et al., "The endocrinology and developmental biology of the prostate," *Endocrine Reviews* 8 (August 1987): 338–362.
6. McNeal, J., "Anatomy and Normal Histology of the Human Prostate," in *Pathology of the Prostate*, eds., C. Foster and D. Bostwick (Philadelphia, Pa.: W.B. Saunders Company, 1998).
7. McNeal, J., E. Redwine, F. Freiha, and T. Stamey, "Zonal distribution of prostatic adenocarcinoma: correlation with histologic pattern and direction of spread," *American Journal of Surgical Pathology* 12, 8 (August 1988): 897–906.
8. Foster, C., and D. Bostwick, eds., *Pathology of the Prostate*. Philadelphia, Pa.: W.B. Saunders Company, 1998.
9. Tobin, A., and J. Dusheck, *Asking about Life*. 3rd ed. Belmont, Calif.: Thomson Learning Inc., 2005.
10. Nobel Foundation. "Nobel Prize" and "Pauling Exhibit." Available online. URL: http://nobelprize.org; http://paulingexhibit.org. Accessed June 5, 2006.
11. Bostwick, D. and W. Sakr, "Prostate intraepithelial neoplasia," in *Pathology of the Prostate*, C. Foster and D. Bostwick, eds. Philadelphia, Pa. :W.B. Saunders Company, 1998.
12. Tobin, A., and J. Dusheck, *Asking about Life*. 3rd ed. Belmont, Calif.: Thomson Learning Inc., 2005.
13. Gleason, D., "Classification of prostatic carcinomas," *Cancer Chemotherapy Reports* 50, no. 3 (March 1966): 125–128.
14. Gleason, D., and G. Mellinger, "Prediction of prognosis for prostatic adenocarcinoma by combined histological grading and clinical staging," *Journal of Urology* 111, no. 1 (January 1974): 58–64.
15. Oesterling, J.E., and M.A. Moyad, *The ABCs of Prostate Cancer: The Book that Could Save Your Life*, Lantham, Md.: Madison Books, 1997.
16. See National Cancer Institute, "Prostate Cancer." Available online. URL: http://www.cancer.gov/cancertopics/types/prostate; for informative websites, see Prostate Cancer Foundation. Available online. URL: http://www.prostatecancer-foundation.org. Accessed June 5, 2006.
17. "Prostate Cancer Brachytherapy (Radioactive Seed Implantation Therapy)." Available online. URL: http://www.emedicine.com/med/topic3147.htm. Accessed June 5, 2006.
18. Nobel Foundation. Available online. URL: http://nobelprize.org/. Accessed June 5, 2006.

19. Kohn, E., and L. Liotta, "Metastasis and Angiogenesis: Molecular Dissection and Novel Applications," in *The Molecular Basis of Cancer*, eds. Mendelsohn, J., Howley, P.M., Israel, M.A.et al.. Philadelphia, Pa.: W.B. Saunders Company, 2001.

20. For an historical account about the discovery of vitamin D, see National Academy of Sciences, "Unraveling the enigma of vitamin D." Available online. URL: http://www.beyonddiscovery.org/content/view.article.asp?a=414. Accessed June 5, 2006.

21. Hollick, M., and M. Jenkins, *The UV Advantage: New Medical Breakthroughs Reveal Powerful Health Benefits from Sun Exposure and Tanning.* New York, N.Y.: Ibooks, 2003.

22. For information on the SELECT trial, see National Cancer Institute, "The SELECT Prostate Cancer Prevention Trial." Available online. URL: http://www.cancer.gov/clinicaltrials/digestpage/SELECT. Accessed June 5, 2006.

23. Hollick, M., and M. Jenkins, *The UV Advantage: New Medical Breakthroughs Reveal Powerful Health Benefits from Sun Exposure and Tanning.* New York, N.Y.: Ibooks, 2003.

24. For information on recommendations on safe levels of Vitamin D_3 and other dietary factors, see Institute of Medicine of the National Academies, Food and Nutrition Board." Available online. URL: http://www.iom.edu/CMS/3788.aspx. Accessed June 5, 2006.

25. Prostate Cancer Foundation. Available online. URL: http://www.prostatecancer-foundation.org. Accessed June 5, 2006.

adrenalectomy—The surgical removal of the adrenal glands

androgen—A steroid hormone made principally by the testes, but also by the adrenal glands and the ovaries. Both men and women have androgen hormones, but men have more than women. (The main male androgen is testosterone.) In men, androgens control sperm maturation, seminal vesicle development, prostate development, muscle growth, facial hair growth, and libido.

antibodies—Proteins produced by the immune system to fight infections.

apoptosis—Also called programmed cell death. This is an active, normal process of the death of a cell.

assay—A procedure, or test, that determines the concentration of a particular part of blood

basal cells—Epithelial cells that act as the interface between the stroma and the luminal epithelial cells

benign prostatic hyperplasia (BPH)—A noncancerous prostate growth

biochemical relapse—A rise in blood **prostate specific antigen (PSA)** levels after therapy indicating a return of the cancer. Most doctors require at least three consecutive PSA tests spanning at least six months to make a diagnosis of prostate cancer relapse.

biopsy—A sample of tissue taken for analysis. For the prostate, the biopsy is taken with a needle inserted into the prostate, usually through the wall of the rectum.

brachytherapy—Also called radioactive seed implants. Pellets of radioactive material are inserted into the prostate gland to kill the tumor.

carcinoma—Cancer of an epithelial tissue. In carcinoma of the prostate, the cancer is characterized by a loss of the basal epithelial layer.

castration—The surgical removal of the testes (see **orchiectomy**)

differentiation—The change of a cell or tissue into a more organized type. An example is the change of a stem cell into a luminal epithelial cell.

digital rectal examination (DRE)—A physical examination of the prostate. The prostate is felt through the wall of the rectum to identify any hardness.

disease progression—The worsening of the disease in severity

duct—A hollow tube lined with epithelium

Glossary

ejaculation—The process of ejection of the sperm and seminal fluid

ejaculatory duct—The tube carrying the sperm and seminal fluid to the urethra

endocrine glands—Organs that secrete hormones to the inside of the body

endocrinology—The study of hormones

enzyme—A substance that carries out a biochemical process. The process can be to break down sugars for energy, to break down fats for energy, to make proteins or to break down proteins.

epidemiology—The study of the causes and transmission of disease

epithelium—A thin layer of tissue made of epithelial cells that covers organs, glands, the genitourinary and gastrointestinal (GI) tracts, as well as other structures

erectile dysfunction—Inability for a man to get an erection.

exocrine gland—An epithelial-lined gland that makes secretions that are secreted to the outside of the body

external beam radiation—Focused radiation to the prostate

extravasation—The process of leaving the blood vessels and entering a tissue

false negative—A negative finding in a screening test when it should be positive. A false negative would lead to the prediction that there is no disease when there really is.

false positive—A positive result in a screening test that is not correct. A false positive would lead to the prediction of disease when there is none.

Gleason grade—A system of classifying prostate cancer based on the glandular structure and pattern in a prostate specimen. There are five Gleason grades, with a Gleason grade 1 prostate being the most like a normal prostate gland (most differentiated) and grade 5 being the least like prostate glands (least differentiated).

Gleason score—An important prognostic tool, the Gleason score is a combination of the first and second most common Gleason grade patterns in a prostate biopsy specimen. The lowest Gleason score is 2 and the highest is 10.

gonadotropin-releasing hormone (GnRH)—A hormone that regulates production of follicle-stimulating hormone and luteinizing hormone. **Sometimes called luteinizing hormone-releasing hormone (LH).**

gray (GY)—The basic unit of radiation treatment. One Gy is defined as 1 joule/kilogram of tissue.

hormone—A signaling molecule made by the body in an endocrine gland that is secreted into the blood and acts on a tissue somewhere else in the body. Hormones control the body's adaptation to the environment.

hormone ablation therapy—Removal or blockage of androgens by surgery, pharmaceuticals, or both in order to prevent or slow the growth of prostate cancer

impotence—The inability to obtain an erection suitable for intercourse

incontinence (urinary)—The inability to control bladder function resulting in leakage of urine

intravasation—The process of entry into the blood system from the local microenvironment

libido—The emotional desire for sexual intercourse

local invasion—The first step of metastasis or spread of cancerous cells beyond the basal layer of the prostate

lumen—An open space in a tissue. In the prostate the lumen contains the prostatic secretions and is surrounded by columnar epithelial cells that make the secretions.

luminal epithelial cells—Epithelial cells that line the lumen of a gland

luteinizing hormone—A hormone produced by the pituitary gland to stimulate the production of testosterone

luteinizing hormone-releasing hormone (LHRH)—Pituitary production of LH is in turn stimulated by GnRH

metastasis—Spread of cancer to other parts of the body

neuroendocrine cells—Epithelial cells located in the basal layer (a layer of undifferentiated cells) of the gland that secretes signaling molecules

nodule—A hardened area of the prostate felt during a digital rectal examination

oncologist—A medical doctor who treats cancer patients. Usually oncologists use hormone therapy and chemotherapy to treat prostate cancer, although urologists also use these treatments.

orchiectomy—The surgical removal of the testes

organ-confined—Prostate cancer that has not spread outside of the prostate

parathyroid hormone (PTH)—A hormone produced by the parathyroid glands, unrelated to the thyroid gland, that is important for regulation of blood calcium levels

pathologist—A person, usually a medical doctor, who studies the changes in a tissue as a result of a disease. These changes are often observed under a microscope. Pathologists often have the final word in the diagnosis of a disease.

prognosis—The prediction of the outcome of a disease

prostate cancer—A malignant growth of cancerous cells in the prostate

prostate specific antigen (PSA)—A protein made by the prostate in very high abundance. PSA is an enzyme important for fertilization. The blood levels of PSA are used as a screening test for prostate cancer. An increase in blood PSA can be caused by BPH, prostatitis, and prostate cancer. Blood PSA levels above 10 ng/ml are usually caused by the presence of prostate cancer. PSA is also used to monitor the success of therapies.

prostatectomy, radical—The surgical removal of the prostate

prostatic intraepithelial neoplasia (PIN)—A change in the microscopic structure of the prostate that is a likely precursor to prostate cancer. Many scientists believe that prostatic intraepithelial neoplasia represents the first visible changes leading to cancer. The cellular changes often seen are enlarged, darkly staining nuclei and a piling up of the luminal cells to fill the lumens. There is always a basal layer present in PIN.

prostatitis—An inflammation of the prostate usually caused by a bacterial, fungal, or viral infection

proteolytic enzyme—An enzyme that breaks down proteins

PTEN (phosphatase and tensin homolog)—A gene that is deleted in 30–40 percent of prostate cancers. The gene product of the PTEN gene prevents prostate cells from growing. When the gene is deleted, the prostate cells can grow faster.

radiation oncologist—A medical doctor who specializes in the use of radiation for the treatment of cancer. The radiation oncologist is the doctor who treats prostate cancer with external beam radiation or **brachytherapy.**

relapse—The recurrence of disease after a period with no evidence of disease

seminal fluid—The secretions of the seminal vesicles, prostate, testes, and vas deferens that make up the fluid necessary for fertilization. About 60 percent of the seminal fluid comes from the seminal vesicles, 30 percent comes from the prostate, and the remainder comes from the testes and vas deferens.

staging—The process of determining the degree that the prostate cancer has spread through the prostate gland and to other parts of the body

stem/progenitor cells—Adult cells located in a tissue that can make the different cell types in the tissue. These cells are thought to have an unlimited potential to grow and divide.

stroma—The cells and tissue components located between epithelial glands

urethra—The duct that travels from the bladder to the outside of the body

urologist—A medical doctor trained in surgery specifically for the urogenital system. For prostate cancer treatment the urologist is the surgeon who performs **prostatectomies** and **orchiectomies**. They are often involved in prostate cancer screening by **digital rectal examination (DRE)** and **prostate specific antigen (PSA)** blood tests. The urologist may also treat prostate cancer with hormone therapy, although the oncologist also uses hormone therapy.

watchful waiting—Informal term for close observation of a person with some signs of prostate cancer, in the absence of any definitive therapy.

Further Reading

American Cancer Society. "Cancer Facts and Figures 2006." Available online. URL: http://www.cancer.org/. Accessed June 5, 2006.

Bostwick, D., and W. Sakr. "Prostate Intraepithelial Neoplasia," in *Pathology of the Prostate*, eds. C. Foster and D. Bostwick. Philadelphia, Pa.:W.B. Saunders Company, 1998.

Cunha, G., A. Donjacour, P. Cooke et al. "The endocrinology and developmental biology of the prostate," *Endocrine Reviews* 8 (August 1987): 338–362.

eMedicine. "Prostate Cancer: Brachytherapy (Radioactive Seed Implantation Therapy)." Available online. URL: http://www.emedicine.com/med/topic3147.htm. Updated March 10, 2005.

Foster, C., and D. Bostwick, eds. *Pathology of the Prostate*. Philadelphia, Pa.: W.B. Saunders Company, 1998.

Gleason, D. "Classification of prostatic carcinomas," *Cancer Chemotherapy Reports* 50, 3 (March 1966): 125–128.

Gleason, D., and G. Mellinger, "Prediction of prognosis for prostatic adenocarcinoma by combined histological grading and clinical staging," *Journal of Urology* 111, 1 (January 1974): 58–64.

Hadley, M. *Endocrinology*. Englewood Cliffs, N.J.: Prentice Hall, 1999.

Hollick, M., and M. Jenkins. *The UV Advantage: New Medical Breakthroughs Reveal Powerful Health Benefits from Sun Exposure and Tanning*. New York: Ibooks, 2003.

Institute of Medicine of the National Academies. "Food and Nutrition Board." Available online. URL: http://www.iom.edu/CMS/3788.aspx. Accessed June 5, 2006.

Kohn, E., and L. Liotta. "Metastasis and Angiogenesis: Molecular Dissection and Novel Applications," in *The Molecular Basis of Cancer*, eds. Mendelsohn, J., Howley, P.M., Israel, M.A. et al. Philadelphia, Pa.: W.B. Saunders Company, 2001.

McNeal, J. "Anatomy and Normal Histology of the Human Prostate," in *Pathology of the Prostate*, eds. C. Foster and D. Bostwick. Philadelphia, Pa.: W.B. Saunders Company, 1998.

McNeal, J., E. Redwine, F. Freiha et al. "Zonal distribution of prostatic adenocarcinoma: correlation with histologic pattern and direction of spread," *American Journal of Surgical Pathology* 12, 8 (August 1988): 897–906.

National Academy of Sciences. "Unraveling the Enigma of Vitamin D." Available online. URL: http://www.beyonddiscovery.org/content/view.article.asp?a=414. Accessed June 5, 2006.

National Cancer Institute. "The SELECT Prostate Cancer Prevention Trial." Available online. URL: http://www.cancer.gov/clinicaltrials/digestpage/SELECT. Accessed June 5, 2006.

Oesterling, J.E., and M.A. Moyad. *The ABCs of Prostate Cancer: The Book that Could Save Your Life.* Lantham, Md.: Madison Books, 1997.

Ries, L., M. Eisner, C. Kosary et al., eds. *SEER Cancer Statistics Review, 1975–2002.* Bethesda, Md.: National Cancer Institute, 2005. Available online. URL: http://seer.cancer.gov/csr/1975_2002/. Accessed June 5, 2006.

Tobin, A., and J. Dusheck. *Asking About Life.* 3rd ed. Belmont, Calif.: Thomson Learning Inc, 2005.

Web sites

Not all information found online is accurate or reliable, so be cautious when using Web sites for research. The Web sites below have been selected as reputable sources of information.

The American Cancer Society
http://www.cancer.org/
This site has up-to-date patient resources for cancer in general.

National Cancer Institute of the National Institutes of Health
http://www.cancer.gov/
http://www.cancer.gov/cancertopics/UnderstandingCancer/genetesting
http://www.cancer.gov/cancertopics/types/prostate
**http://www.cancer.gov/cancertopics/prevention-genetics-causes/
 prostate**
http://www.cancer.gov/clinicaltrials
Because of its extensive resources, the NCI site is the place to start researching prostate cancer.

Prostate Cancer Foundation
http://www.prostatecancerfoundation.org/
This is a nonprofit organization established to increase research on prostate cancer and to act as a patient advocacy group.

PubMed, National Library of Medicine and National Institutes of Health
http://www.ncbi.nlm.nih.gov/entrez/query.fcgi?DB=pubmed
This is a very helpful search tool jointly sponsored by the National Library of Medicine and the National Institutes of Health.

USToo
http://www.ustoo.com
This is a network of men and families with prostate cancer that acts as a patient advocacy group and support group. The site offers a range of useful information

Index

Index

Index

About the Author

Scott D. Cramer, Ph.D., is an associate professor in the Department of Cancer Biology, Wake Forest University School of Medicine. He is currently researching the molecular dissection of signaling pathways in prostatic cells, the identification of prostate progenitor or stem cells, and understanding epithelial-stromal interactions in normal and abnormal ductal morphogenesis.